Malnutrition
What Can Be Done?

A World Bank Publication

Malnutrition
What Can Be Done?

Lessons from World Bank Experience

Alan Berg

Published for The World Bank
The Johns Hopkins University Press
Baltimore and London

Copyright © 1987 by the International Bank
for Reconstruction and Development / THE WORLD BANK
1818 H Street, N.W., Washington, D.C. 20433, U.S.A.
All rights reserved
Manufactured in the United States of America
First printing August 1987
The Johns Hopkins University Press
Baltimore, Maryland 21211, U.S.A.

The findings, interpretations, and conclusions expressed in this study are
the results of sectoral and project analysis and research supported by the
World Bank, but they are entirely those of the author and should not be
attributed in any manner to the World Bank, to its affiliated organizations,
or to members of its Board of Executive Directors or the countries they
represent.

Library of Congress Cataloging-in-Publication Data

Berg, Alan D.
  Malnutrition: what can be done?

  ''Published for the World Bank.''
  Bibliography: p.
  Includes index.
  1. Nutrition policy—Developing countries. 2. Diet
—Developing countries. I. International Bank for
Reconstruction and Development. II. Title.
TX360.5.B47   1987   363.8'56'091724   87-45493
ISBN 0-8018-3553-4 (pbk.)

Contents

Acknowledgments

THE PROJECTS in this book reflect work in a number of countries by many hundreds of people, unfortunately too many to all name here. Among those deserving special mention from the governments that undertook the projects were Adinuggroho Asrarudin, Bertoldo Kruse Grande de Arruda, Vital Didonet, Eduardo Kertesz, Susan Mathew, Sonya Rahardjo, Anuradha Khati Rajivan, Magdalena Rodrigues, Elena Silva, R. Socbekll, Soekirman, I. G. Tarwotjo, Tomas Uribe-Mosquera, Migel Urrutia, and Girija Vaidyanathan.

Those on the World Bank staff who were primarily involved were Bansi Amla, Samir Basta, Rolf Carriere, James Greene, Carmen Hamann, John Kevany, Emmerich Schebeck, S. Venkitaramanan, and Neil Wilkie. Among the large number of consultants who assisted in the design, execution, or evaluation of these projects, particularly noteworthy were the contributions of David Boianovsky, Sol Chafkin, Sylvester da Cunha, David Dapice, Alberto Carvahlo da Silva, M. S. W. Gizi, Marcia Griffiths, Jean-Pierre Habicht, Lukas Hendrata, Guillermo Herrera, E. J. R. Heyward, Abraham Horwitz, Michael Latham, Richard K. Manoff, Reynaldo Martorell, Nirmala Murthy, James Pines, Per Pinstrup-Andersen, Selo Soemardjan, and Ewen Thomson.

The books draws on a review of the World Bank's work in nutrition prepared for the Bank's senior management. Many people contributed to that internal report. Background papers were written by George Beaton, Lauren Chester, T. J. Ho, Joanne Leslie, Robert Muscat, James Pines, and Per Pinstrup-Andersen. A working group consisting of Stephen Denning, James Greene, Dean Jamison, Anthony Measham, and Emmerich Schebeck provided insight and general guidance during the preparation of the review, and deliberations of the World Bank's Population, Health, and Nutrition Department at a retreat on the subject contributed to the final shape. Subsequent discussions with Fred Sai were also important.

The perceptions and contributions of Susan Brems, James Greene, Shlomo Reutlinger, and Richard Skolnik are felt throughout. Ms. Brems was instrumental in helping to transform the report into a book.

Sonia Ainsworth, Patricia Coogan, and Amelia Menciano all typed portions of the book at one stage or another; Lisa Collins served as research assistant; and Alice M. Carroll edited the manuscript for publication.

Author's Note

As THIS BOOK was going to press, updated information became available on the costs and effects of India's Tamil Nadu Integrated Nutrition Project (TINP), which is discussed frequently in these pages. Monitoring and evaluation data through early 1987 confirm the high probability that the project has caused a substantial decline in serious and severe malnutrition.

According to the monitoring data for the 9,000 villages in the program, 17 to 24 percent of the children weighed less than 70 percent of the median weight for their age, based on Indian standards, at the time the project began. By early 1987 between 7 and 10 percent of the children were below that level, a decline of about 58 percent. The ranges reflect differences among districts, but data collected separately from all six districts in the project point in the same direction and are of the same general magnitude. Another analysis using a different baseline, which is now being undertaken by the state's Department of Evaluation and Applied Research, suggests a decline of about 40 percent. By any of these measures, the impact has been large. Declines of these magnitudes have never before been observed in an operational setting and certainly not in an equivalent period of time.

Preliminary findings suggest that infant mortality also may have declined noticeably in project areas. The data are limited, however, and require considerable further analysis before firm conclusions can be drawn. A clearer picture is likely to be obtained from the final evaluation report scheduled for completion in late 1987.

The number of children participating in monthly weighing sessions remained above 90 percent in those areas covered by the 9,000 community nutrition workers and in Madurai, the initial district, above 95 percent. Of the children weighed, 28 percent required special feeding at any one time and 98 percent of those eligible for the feeding participated in that part of the program. The dropout rate from the feeding program was 2.2 percent. Fewer than five feeding days a month were missed by 97 percent of the children who remained in the program. Of those who participated in the feeding, 61 percent gained sufficient weight to graduate from the program after three months and a further 17 percent graduated after six months.

The most recent evaluation data indicate that costs are somewhat lower than those presented in chapter 3. The annual per capita cost is Rs10 (or US$0.81, rather than the $1.02 reported in table 3-1), compared with Rs18.4 for comparable services in the state in the Integrated Child Development Scheme (ICDS). The cost of expanding the Tamil Nadu Integrated Nutrition Project to cover the full state would account for less than 0.5 percent of the state gross domestic product (compared with more than 1.0 percent for ICDS) and 2.5 percent of the state revenue budget (ICDS is 5.4 percent).

ICDS in Tamil Nadu appears to have been responsible for a 20 to 25 percent reduction in cases of advanced malnutrition, an impressive achievement of itself. If the reduction in malnutrition achieved by TINP is assumed to be 50 percent (the approximate midpoint between the monitoring and evaluation data), TINP delivers about twice the benefit for slightly more than half the cost. This finding, which is fairly robust for various definitions of costs, suggests that a well-managed and targeted program is able to reduce serious and severe malnutrition more than a less-focused program, and at a significantly lower cost.

August 1987

1 | The Problem with Malnutrition

MALNUTRITION is a problem that defies pat solution. It has many roots: inadequate food supply, limited purchasing power, poor health conditions, and incomplete knowledge about nutrition. These causes often combine in different ways over time and place. In any combination, they are often aggravated by uncertain political commitment. This makes it difficult for government workers who must develop strategies and programs to combat malnutrition, and for foreign assistance agencies that try to help them.

Adding to the complexity is the lack of an organizational locus for carrying out such programs, because nutrition is not a sector in the conventional sense. Rather, it is a condition, like unemployment. Solutions must cut across disciplines and organization charts. Government officials have no ministry or department of nutrition to turn to. Nor does any United Nations organization have a primary mandate to help countries contend with malnutrition.

As such, malnutrition is everybody's business but nobody's main responsibility. In most countries, the scant energies devoted to it in policy and operations are what remain after agencies have addressed their primary missions. Those limited efforts, when they fail to meet the nutrition needs of the population, often are written off as inappropriate—sometimes even as too expensive. And malnutrition persists.

Yet officials in a number of countries have continued to grapple with what can be done about malnutrition. Their efforts have become more urgent as more is learned about its far-reaching effects.

In the mid-1970s, the World Bank began to explore how it might contribute to these efforts to improve nutrition. In discussions about the appropriateness of a role for the Bank, two questions were posed. Was malnutrition a development problem and therefore one the Bank

1

should address? If so, were there feasible things that could be done about it, particularly things that the Bank was suited to do?

The answer to the first question appeared to be yes. The problem of malnutrition was recognized to be substantial, and the effectiveness of nutrition measures in reducing the number of deaths, decreasing the severity of childhood infection, and preventing forms of blindness, anemia-induced lethargy, and other handicaps was reasonably well established and was in itself regarded as sufficient justification for investment in better nutrition.

Recognition of the consequences of malnutrition for national development was growing. Researchers were calculating the costs of inadequate diet and related illness on the physical development, learning ability, capacity to work, behavior, and well-being of large segments of populations. Nutritionists were beginning to investigate the compounded effects of childhood handicaps on the physical well-being and earning capacities of adults. Evidence was pointing to a considerable human and economic waste caused by inadequate nutrition. In short, malnutrition was beginning to be seen both as a cause and as an effect of underdevelopment.[1]

The answer to the question of whether there were things that could be done about malnutrition, and on which the Bank could help, was more problematic. While there was little doubt that over the long run nutrition could be improved through increases in per capita income of the poor (which depend on national economic growth and the pattern of that growth), in most countries such change was slow. World Bank research later showed that in many places per capita income was not likely to increase enough within a generation to solve the problems of the currently malnourished. Per capita income increases slowly for the poor, and their food energy (or calorie) intake rises less than half as rapidly.[2]

Moreover, an examination of per capita calorie consumption in ninety developing countries showed that during the 1970s consumption declined in twenty-six. In another twenty, the annual compound growth in consumption was less than 0.5 percent, and in some it was at a virtual standstill (in Brazil, for example, it was 0.2 percent). Those numbers were national averages, so to the extent that income distribution was skewed against the poor, the figures understated the problem.[3] In the poorer countries, the near-term outlook appeared grim, an expectation that has been corroborated by the events of the early 1980s.

Attempts were being made to improve the food picture in the 1970s through the most traditional method—increased production. This no doubt is the main need in countries where large portions of the poor have access to land. In those cases increases in food production and consumption can be nearly synonymous.

But for vast proportions of the world's malnourished, increased production is not the primary need. More than half of those in need in most countries are families of landless agricultural laborers, farmers with landholdings too small to be reached by rural development programs, small-scale fishermen, and unemployed urban workers. The impressive increases in food production by many countries since the late 1960s have demonstrated that supply alone is not a sufficient response. India, for example, produces substantial food surpluses while malnutrition persists throughout the country. Even at the height of India's Green Revolution, when agricultural production in the Punjab became a model for that part of the world, the poor nutrition status of low-income people in the Punjab did not improve.[4] Similarly, malnutrition continues to be widespread today in Indonesia, Pakistan, and the Philippines—all countries that are considered "self-sufficient" in food grains—and in Bangladesh, which is nearly self-sufficient. These countries, along with China—another dramatic deficit-to-surplus turnaround with some continuing malnutrition—constitute over two-thirds of the total population of the low-income and lower-middle-income countries.

Still other attempts to deal with malnutrition were coming through the health system; feeding programs, vitamin and mineral supplements, and nutrition education increasingly were being provided in health centers. Immunization and other steps to improve the general state of health also could have favorable effects on nutrition, just as improved nutrition could enhance health. But nutrition deficiencies in some developing countries were so vast and health systems generally so limited in coverage that malnutrition was not being significantly alleviated through this route.

In fact, few central ministries had the resources, outreach, or organizational capacity to mount substantial nutrition efforts. Most programs whose objectives were deliberately concerned with nutrition emphasized face-to-face techniques. Mass techniques, such as fortification of centrally processed foods, subsidization of consumer food purchases to improve nutrition, application of social marketing methods, including nutrition education through mass media, and adjustment of agricultural price policies to favor nutrition effects, were rarely employed in developing countries.

Moreover, for the most part those government actions that were undertaken were not directed to the poorest segments of the population or to the most nutritionally vulnerable members of those groups—children six months to three years of age and pregnant and nursing women. Although nutrition problems are important among people of all ages and both sexes, very young children and their mothers are generally most at risk.

An understanding of the character and scope of a country's nutrition deficiencies is a basic requirement for undertaking a mass effort to correct them. But most developing countries in the mid-1970s were collecting little data on food consumption or spending patterns, on households with malnourished mothers, or even on nutrition status. And despite substantial public institutional feeding programs, particularly school feeding programs, little evaluation of their benefits was taking place.

The limitations of past approaches and the identification of new and largely untested approaches suggested a range of feasible actions for exploration: expanding food supplies in ways that would benefit the poor, with attention to what is grown, who grows it, and what is stored; accelerating increases in the incomes of the poor; improving marketing systems and adjusting pricing policies to benefit the poor consumer without destroying producers' incentives; introducing more targeting into feeding programs; promoting beneficial nutrition practices, including attention to the special consumption needs of women and children; improving health and environmental conditions (by providing safe water, sanitation, immunization, and treatment for diarrhea); and setting up large-scale programs to solve problems caused by specific vitamin and mineral deficiencies. The answer to the second question was, then, a qualified yes. There were things that might be done about malnutrition.

It was in this environment that the World Bank set out to work with governments in an effort to understand malnutrition better and test ways of reducing its incidence.[a] The Bank's Board of Executive Di-

a. In this effort *malnutrition* was defined as the pathological condition brought about by the inadequacy of one or more of the essential nutrients that the body cannot make but that are necessary for survival, for growth and reproduction, and for the capacity to work, learn, and function in society. People whose diets fall short of standard international levels of intake for these nutrients are said to suffer from malnutrition. Because the dominant malnutrition problem in large populations is insufficient intake rectors decided to finance the implementation and evaluation of certain largely experimental actions that appeared to have high priority. In short, a learning-by-doing strategy was adopted. At the same time, the Bank would support training, other forms of institution building, and longer-term analyses aimed at more sophisticated operations later.

In 1980 the Bank's senior management decided that efforts should also be made to incorporate nutrition concerns in agricultural and rural development projects and that improvement in nutrition status should become an objective and part of the design of appropriate health projects. The scope and complexity of malnutrition suggested that an effort be made in the Bank's economic and sector analyses of countries seeking aid to improve understanding of the nature and extent of the problem—where in the chain of nutrition events the weakest links were that needed addressing and ways nutrition might better be integrated into country operations—and, to the extent possible, to identify suitable actions. One to three countries in each of the Bank's six regions would be analyzed in depth. Where freestanding nutrition projects—those directed primarily at nutrition objectives—appeared to be the most appropriate mechanism to achieve a stated nutrition objective, they would be undertaken. And the Bank would continue to sponsor operational research into nutrition problems and efforts to alleviate them. The thrust of the Bank's nutrition program would be in its areas of particular advantage: drawing the attention of officials to problems, assisting in planning, furthering the development of rigorous project analysis, and providing enough resources to make significant interventions possible.

Some areas did not receive the attention intended, and in others the Bank was unable to carry through on what it had hoped to do. But much has been learned from the Bank's first attempts to deal with malnutrition. And along the way quite unexpected findings have emerged, a few of them even refuting conventional notions about development. The Bank's experience suggests the following:

▸ Although malnutrition is closely linked to a country's level of economic development, nutrition improvements need not await that

---

of food energy (which for many people also commonly carries over to inadequate protein), energy-protein malnutrition, a broad term encompassing deficiencies of both calories and protein, has been the principal target of the activities of the World Bank. Other deficiencies, particularly of vitamin A, iron, and iodine, have also been of concern. (For greater detail, see appendix E of the work cited in note 2 to this chapter.)

development. In fact, substantial improvements can be made even during periods of economic decline, as evidenced in the project in the Indian state of Tamil Nadu.

- Large food programs—ranging from consumer food subsidies to child feeding through institutions—need not be prohibitive in cost. In Brazil, Colombia, and India, experience shows that such food programs can be targeted to the needy in ways that push per capita costs to much lower levels than in earlier programs.

- Even though malnutrition is closely related to poverty, malnutrition sometimes is not bound by family income. This is seen from Bank analysis in countries as diverse as Brazil, Côte d'Ivoire, Indonesia, and the Yemen Arab Republic.

- Women's lack of schooling need not pose the insurmountable constraint to improved nutrition that it is widely believed to pose. Although formal education for women has many important benefits, the Indonesian experience demonstrates that education level does not define how much women are able to learn or achieve in safeguarding or improving their children's nutrition, if the women receive highly specific messages, appropriately tailored and delivered. The Indonesian project also demonstrates for the first time in a large operational setting that nutrition education alone can do much to improve nutrition status.

- Vitamin and mineral deficiencies may be caused by a rapid shift from traditional, locally produced grains such as millet and sorghum to polished rice and refined wheat, both often imported (such processing causes loss of certain natural nutrients). Sector analyses in Nigeria, Zambia, and Zimbabwe have exposed such shifts in consumption, which should be regarded as potential nutrition dangers.

- Improved nutrition appears to affect the capacity to work and learn. Significant relations between nutrition status and worker productivity have been found in research undertaken in Indonesia and Kenya. And Bank research in Brazil, China, and Nepal has shown a link between nutrition and school attendance and performance that will affect future earning capacity and contribution to national growth.

- Social and psychological dependence among recipients need not be an inevitable outcome of feeding programs. A nutrition program for close to 1 million children and women in Tamil Nadu has used new techniques that avoid this danger.

• By increasing efficiencies in the food marketing system, it is possible to reduce substantially the prices that low-income families must pay for food. That is a particularly significant finding from the Brazil project.

Just as much has been learned about what *not* to do.

This book discusses what has and has not been achieved in the efforts the Bank has undertaken with governments in nutrition. It does not attempt to survey the large body of work done by other governments, nongovernmental organizations, and donors active in nutrition. Except for a few references, the material here covers work done before 1985. Four large nutrition projects, which were the first substantial nutrition actions the Bank took part in, are described in chapter 2; the costs, affordability, and cost-effectiveness of the programs and some of their design characteristics are discussed in chapters 3 and 4. Chapter 5 surveys fifty-seven nutrition actions that were components or subcomponents of other Bank-assisted projects, and chapter 6 reviews the content of some seventy-five pieces of nutrition-related research supported by the Bank and nutrition analyses in the Bank's economic and sector work. The lessons gleaned from the limited experience in this field are reviewed in chapter 7. Thoughts on future action, described in chapter 8, may be useful in designing new programs.

The potential applicability of nutrition project experience to the design and support of structural adjustment programs merits particular note. This relatively new form of financing is intended to make it easier for borrowing countries to implement reforms intended to alleviate debt-servicing and balance of payments problems. Many of the areas frequently slated for reform—such as eliminating or reducing consumer food price subsidies—impinge directly or indirectly on nutrition. Unless properly planned, such programs may have nutritionally negative repercussions, particularly in the short run.

In addressing the challenge of how to curtail expenditures but protect vulnerable groups, the targeting lessons of Bank nutrition projects may be instructive. The Bank's Operations Evaluation Department, whose mandate is to assess operational work by independent examination, recognized in its 1986 annual review of projects that the lessons of success with targeted consumer food subsidy programs in Bank nutrition projects are especially important for the analysis of structural adjustment. The targeting experiences discussed in chapters 2, 7, and 8 can help guide program design that enhances nutrition for the poor or, at least, cushions them from the shock of dismantling food subsidies or other adjustments.

Addressing the underlying causes of poverty remains a vitally important development objective. But the time required to reach the most impoverished and the immediacy of the malnutrition problem argue for a continuing direct attack on nutrition deficiencies as well. The findings reported here suggest that efficacious and affordable measures are at hand.

2 | Projects Directed at Malnutrition

THE WORLD BANK began its participation in direct nutrition interventions in the mid-1970s. Its emphasis in four projects initiated between 1977 and 1980 was on understanding and dealing with the administrative, economic, and political realities of such efforts. The four projects that the Bank took part in were all in countries that were principal recipients of Bank assistance—Brazil, Colombia, India, and Indonesia. During the years the nutrition projects were initiated, these countries accounted for about one-third of all Bank lending. Despite economic growth, all four continued to face significant problems of malnutrition. In some cases economic development had bypassed a large portion of the population. In others the problem was so vast that decades of substantial equitable growth would be required to meet the needs of the population.

Each of the nutrition projects was designed to test different approaches to sometimes different nutrition deficiencies. However, they had certain common features (see table 2-1). All included one or more components for institution building and several operational components, among them usually delivery of nutrition services through the health care system, some form of supplementary feeding or food subsidy program, and nutrition education. The three projects that got under way in 1977 and 1978 were multisectoral, with agricultural, water supply and sanitation, and food marketing components sometimes added to more direct nutrition actions. The fourth—which can be viewed as a second-generation project—was designed to concentrate on fewer actions.

The extent of the health and malnutrition problems that the four projects addressed differed widely. Though average daily food consumption appeared to be quite reasonable in Brazil, Colombia, and Indonesia, a substantial proportion of households in all three coun-

9

Table 2-1. Scope of World Bank–Assisted Nutrition Projects
in Brazil, Colombia, India, and Indonesia

Description	Brazil	Colombia	India	Indonesia
Region	Northeast	Seven neediest of 22 departments	Tamil Nadu state	Pilot areas in several provinces
Date[a]	1977–83	1978–83	1980–87	1977–83
Project cost (millions of U.S. dollars)				
Total	72	87	66	26
Bank loan	19	25	32[b]	13
Components				
Institution-building (including training)	x	x	x	x
Supplementary feeding	x	—	x	x
Food subsidies	x	x	—	—
Health services with nutrition	x	x	x	x
Nutrition education	x	x	x	x
Anemia control	—	x	x	x
Small-scale food production (including family gardens)	x	x	—	x
Food technology (including reduction of food loss) and quality control	x	x	—	x
Water supply and sanitation	—	x	—	· —
Food marketing	x	x	—	—

x Included.
— Not included.
a. Implementation periods include extensions.
b. Amount is a credit from the International Development Association, an affiliate of the World Bank.
Source: World Bank data.

tries undoubtedly consumed far less than the required level of food.[a] Weaning-age children and pregnant and lactating women probably suffered doubly because of the way food was distributed within families. In India, where per capita food supply was lower, it is likely that an even larger fraction of households suffered substantial consumption shortfalls.

The infant mortality rate, which is strongly influenced by the health and nutrition status of mothers, was nearly twice as high in India as in Colombia. The child death rate, considered to be a strong indicator of the prevalence of malnutrition among children one to four years old, was also high in all four countries, but four times as high in India as in Colombia.

The Four Projects

The first of the projects to go into action was the Brazil Nutrition Research and Development Project, which started in January 1977. The main objectives of the project were to develop and test techniques for countering malnutrition among children of preschool age and pregnant and lactating women in low-income families, to provide the government with basic information and the institutional and manpower capabilities to develop and carry out nutrition policies, and to develop and produce certain inexpensive food products of high nutritional value.

Although the Brazilian government had no nutrition policy, a large number of mostly small nutrition activities had been under way for some years, and a National Food and Nutrition Institute (INAN) was being established as a focal point for nutrition work. Information gathered in the highly experimental nutrition project—through special studies and evaluation of field components—would be used to design and conduct a national nutrition program. Most of the studies and all of the evaluations were to be undertaken by local research

---

a. Income distribution was particularly skewed in Brazil, where in 1972 the poorest 20 percent of households had only 2 percent of household income, while the top 20 percent had 67 percent. In both India and Indonesia in 1976 the poorest 20 percent had 7 percent of household income and the top 20 percent had 49 percent. No comparable figures are available for Colombia. See World Bank, *World Development Report 1982* (New York: Oxford University Press, 1982).

centers. INAN was responsible for coordinating, monitoring, research, and evaluation.

The second of the projects, the Indonesia Nutrition Development Project, began in April 1977. That project got off to a slow start, in part because it was the first collaborative effort between the Ministry of Health and the Bank, and differences between government and Bank financial procedures had to be reconciled. Furthermore, the government's experience in nutrition had been largely limited to an ineffective Applied Nutrition Program. And there was a shortage of trained nutritionists and persons versed in nutrition concepts.

The objectives of the Indonesia project were to develop measures to improve nutrition status, to develop personnel and institutions capable of setting up and managing large nutrition programs, and to aid the government in the formulation and execution of a national program. Project funds were dedicated more or less equally to institution-building activities and to action programs directed at improving calorie and protein consumption among small children, ameliorating iron-deficiency anemia, and changing practices that adversely influenced nutrition status.

The Colombia Integrated Nutrition Improvement Project, which got under way in March 1978, was the outcome of that government's broad, carefully planned strategy to fight malnutrition.[1] The comprehensive set of programs that were to underpin the effort ran the gamut from helping small landholders increase production of basic foods to instituting a market mechanism that allowed those living in absolute poverty to improve their food consumption. The strategy included both an integrated rural development program and a nutrition program (PAN) drawn up by the National Planning Department. The former included previously unavailable assistance to farmers, including an ensured market for increased crops, which would reduce the farmers' risk in obtaining credit. The market would be ensured because under PAN the government would provide subsidized weaning foods and other processed food supplements to families of landless laborers and other malnourished poor. Manufacture of these foods was designed to decrease reliance on internationally donated food aid. The coupons that entitled the nutritionally most vulnerable groups to the subsidy would be available through primary health care posts, thus encouraging the use of growth monitoring and other basic nutrition and health services. To reduce nutrient losses through diarrhea, potable water and latrines were to be provided, and food quality control was to be instituted. Nutrition education was to be expanded and, finally, the increased production and consumption of homegrown food were to be encouraged.

The objectives of the nutrition project, which were linked to the PAN portion of the strategy, were "to improve nutrition, living standards and the productive capacity of 1.8 million Colombians," to monitor and evaluate the project's activities, which were integrated at both the community and the national levels, and to strengthen the program's managerial base. Its prospects were good, for it was being executed through the strong National Planning Department, and the nutrition program was a major plank of the presidential platform.

Lessons from the first three Bank-assisted nutrition projects led to a decision to make the fourth, the Tamil Nadu Integrated Nutrition Project (known locally as TINP), less complicated. In 1977 the government of India had asked for assistance to improve nutrition conditions in Tamil Nadu. A pioneering nutrition systems study, started nearly a decade before with assistance from the U.S. Agency for International Development, had established a strong data base for the project and an understanding about the many determinants of malnutrition in Tamil Nadu. The state government of Tamil Nadu also had a long-standing commitment to improving nutrition and to social development generally.

A main purpose of the Tamil Nadu government's project was to bring efficiencies to existing efforts. Twenty-five nutrition programs were already operating in the state and were seen to have relatively modest effect. Collectively, they reached fewer than 10 percent of the state's preschool children.

From the Bank's and other donors' experience, it was decided that the implementation period for the Tamil Nadu project should be six years, rather than the four years projected for the earlier projects. The last year would be devoted to a major evaluation of the project's impact. To accelerate decisionmaking, a committee of senior civil servants, chaired by the chief secretary of the state government, was made responsible for overseeing the project. Day-to-day coordination, monitoring, and overall budgeting would be carried out by an autonomous Project Coordination Office working closely with implementing agencies, mainly the Directorates of Social Welfare and

Health and the state government's Department of Evaluation and
Applied Research.

The project, which got under way in August 1980, concentrated
exclusively on children six to thirty-six months old and expectant and
nursing women. Children under three accounted for an estimated 90
percent of preschool deaths in the state, with malnutrition being a
major or associated cause of three-quarters of those deaths. The
project employed a sensitive but practical growth monitoring system
to identify children who were nutritionally at risk; administered
highly selective, short-term supplementary feeding to help those children reach an acceptable pattern of weight gain; similarly provided
food supplements to mothers at risk (criteria included, for example,
whether the mother had a malnourished child or had lost one); involved the mothers in the process through a comprehensive communications program incorporating both personal instruction and mass
media; and featured rigorously managed information and evaluation
systems.

Project Content

The four projects contained programs that showed great promise,
programs that went astray because their objectives were bent to other
purposes, and programs that proved too ambitious to realize under
the circumstances. They are full of lessons on the potentials and
pitfalls of specific nutrition-oriented actions, the capacity of international, national, and local institutions to undertake them, and the
possibility for their use in other settings.

Targeting Food Distribution, Supplementation, and Subsidy Programs

Consumer food subsidy programs in Brazil and Colombia and feeding programs in Brazil, India, and Indonesia used a variety of approaches to identify the at-risk populations and to target nutrition
services. The emphasis on targeting is an important break from the
past, when mass coverage was the norm. The main lesson is that
some forms of targeting are feasible and in some cases do indeed
lower costs.

SUBSIDIES IN BRAZIL. One component of Brazil's project was tar-geted by household income and was designed to test the effects on nutrition of different levels of and approaches to consumer food sub-sidies. The program, known as PINS, initially distributed coupons to 10,000 families below a specified income threshold. The operation was supervised locally (through large government-owned super-markets), as was the evaluation of this component. A 1982 evaluation by Roberto Nunes of the growth of children in four subsidy groups (subsidies of 60, 45, and 30 percent of costs and a 45 percent subsidy that required a monthly medical examination to qualify) showed that the percentage of malnourished children in each group was signifi-cantly lower (from 11 to 37 percent) than would be expected without the program.[2] The findings were consistent across age groups and by different measures of nutrition status. (The evaluation did not control for the effects of self-selection or for socioeconomic factors.) The re-duction in malnutrition (which coincided with a reduction in buying power of the general population) "provides fairly strong evidence" that the intervention had a significant, positive effect on the nutrition status of the intended beneficiaries.[3]

The PINS dropout rate varied significantly with subsidy level—26 percent of those receiving the highest subsidy dropped out after twelve months, 75 percent of those receiving the lowest, 46 percent of those receiving the mid-level, and 63 percent in the mid-level group required to have medical examinations. The evaluations revealed that those needing help most could not always put together the cash required to take advantage of the subsidy (because of extra paper-work, the supermarkets limited purchase of the subsidized foods to once a fortnight). And distances to the supermarkets were so great that many families needed taxis to take the groceries home. From this analysis the studies suggested the value of targeting by neighbor-hood: it would be better to offer subsidies to all families in carefully targeted geographic areas with a very high percentage of low-income households than attempt to distribute coupons to families chosen by level of income (income reporting, in any case, proved to be very arbitrary). They also showed the program would have greater impact if the subsidized food was sold regularly in small neighborhood shops.

Building on these lessons, the PINS program was modified to reach very low-income neighborhoods without requiring coupons or down payments. Commonly consumed basic foods were subsidized for all customers of many registered small neighborhood stores in selected poverty areas. The value of the subsidy was adjusted so that more was given at those times of the year when food prices were highest. Any leakage of benefits to those not in need (observed by Bank staff to be very small in the pilot project in Recife) was expected to be considerably less expensive than the cumbersome coupon program with its heavy costs for bookkeeping and related administration.[b] The revised system, known as PROAB, made possible frequent purchases of small quantities.

SUBSIDIES IN COLOMBIA. In Colombia distribution of food coupons was central to the strategy developed for the nutrition project. All 930 *municipios* (the principal subdivision of the twenty-four *departamentos* that make up Colombia) were ranked by levels of income and access to public services, and coupons were made available in the poorest 30 percent. Further targeting was achieved by limiting this food subsidy in those areas to households in which there was a child under five or a pregnant or nursing woman. The coupons could be used at food stores in partial payment for a selection of twenty-three processed foods of high nutritional value.[c] Through the coupons, the program aimed at contributing an additional 10 percent to the monthly income of households whose income stood at 30 percent of the national average.

The careful targeting of beneficiaries helped to keep down the costs of Colombia's program and strengthened the effectiveness of nutrition education by focusing attention on those with special nutrition needs and by encouraging consumption of certain nutritious weaning foods. At the peak of the program in 1981, coupons were being used by an estimated 140,000 beneficiaries, 68 percent of the targeted pop-

b. Apparently a combination of discomfort and inconvenience kept affluent nonresidents from buying at subsidized shops in poor neighborhoods. Retailers observed restrictions on price and quantities that could be purchased, because infractions could (and, in a few well-publicized, early cases, did) cause revocation of license to participate in the program, and nonparticipation could mean losing customers who would also purchase nonsubsidized items.

c. Manufacture of these foods was intended to favor local agribusinesses, which were given access to credit and other types of assistance. Participating businesses were subject to price competition and strict quality control. Subsidization of fresh foods was also envisioned, but the program was dismantled before that activity got under way. See Consuelo Uribe, "Limitations and Constraints of Colombia's Food and Nutrition Plan PAN," *Food Policy*, vol. 2, no. 1 (February 1986), pp. 47–70.

ulation, which Bank consultants regarded as a respectable achievement for an unusual and complicated program that involved the private food sector working with government agencies. Most beneficiaries participated irregularly, partly because they lacked cash to buy their full share of subsidized foods. Price inflation caused the real value of the subsidy to drop by about one-third over the life of the program.

Very little leakage or fraudulent use was apparent in the Colombia program. Mario Ochoa's study of the program indicated that administrative costs as a percentage of the value of the coupon subsidy declined over five years from 41.7 percent to 1.8 percent. Meanwhile, coupons redeemed rose from 16.1 percent to 95.8 percent of coupons distributed.[4] The coupons seem to have been better accepted in urban than in rural areas (75 percent of eligible urban households collected their coupons and 90 percent of the coupons were exchanged, compared with 30 percent and less than 50 percent, respectively, in rural areas).

Evaluation of the PAN program in Cauca, Colombia's second poorest departamento, showed that—with allowances made for family income, the value of food stamps received, and other factors—participation induced a substantial increase in family food expenditures. (Cauca's results understate the benefits of the PAN program, because a smaller percentage of food coupons was redeemed there than for the program as a whole.) The value of food stamps as a proportion of total income in Cauca was not associated with changes in food consumption, however, so that improved nutrition knowledge and awareness may have been principally responsible for the changes. Regression analysis shows that visits to a health center that distributed coupons were associated with improved food consumption, which increased on the order of 300 calories per person per day. How the increased consumption was distributed within the family and how it affected the growth of target individuals are not clear.[5]

SUPPLEMENTATION IN INDIA. Targeting in direct feeding programs was best achieved in the Tamil Nadu project, which covered rural areas of the six districts where the most inadequate caloric consumption in the state was found. These districts alone represented a population of 17.2 million—more than the total national populations of twenty-three of the thirty-four countries in the low-income category within which the World Bank classifies India.

Within the project areas targeting was by age and need. Nutrition care was based on weighing all children six to thirty-six months old at community nutrition centers and (for those children who did not get to the centers) in households and plotting their weight on individual growth charts to determine the velocity of gain.[d] Children whose weight gain over a specified time fell below standard were enrolled in a ninety-day supplementation program that included daily feeding at the center and intensive counseling of mothers. Once children gained weight adequately, they were taken off the supplementary regime. A principal goal of the program was to minimize the risk of long-term dependence on the food assistance. Children who did not respond to the supplementation were referred to the health services.

Village workers motivated by good training, good supervision, and good project support materials kept participation rates at over 90 percent in the growth monitoring program, even when the majority of the children received no food supplement. About 25 percent of monitored children required short-term food supplementation at any one time, and 95 percent of those who needed it participated. Of those who received supplements, 65 percent showed adequate growth velocity in 90 days, and a further 15 percent in 120 days; the rest required extended supplementation.[e] By targeting feeding to the needy—when they needed it—the food cost was significantly below that of most feeding programs for children of preschool age.

Community enthusiasm for the program was reflected in the formation of groups of women in nearly all project villages who took on the task of preparing the food supplement. The use of a wheat-based product, prepared from inexpensive and locally available ingredients as a traditional snack food (*laddu*), reduced the tendency of families to view the supplement as a substitute for the rice-based diet at home (many Tamil families do not consider food that does not contain rice to be a meal). And while the children were on the supplementation

d. Velocity of weight gain, tried as an indicator in Tamil Nadu for the first time on a large scale, proved to be a more sensitive measure of nutritional adequacy than the commonly used weight for age. The Tamil Nadu project also demonstrated that growth monitoring, when properly practiced (and linked to nutrition education and, when necessary, selective feeding), can be a powerful instrument for child health. The value of growth monitoring, in the absence of such models, has been an issue of some contention in the nutrition community.

e. Some 85 percent of all children in the project required supplementation at least once, indicating that most of these children are at risk of malnutrition and suggesting that a wide socioeconomic range is affected.

program, mothers seemed not to reduce the intake of those children at home, apparently at least partly to avoid embarrassment if the children did not show a weight gain.

The effects of the program appear to be dramatic. The portion of children in the program requiring feeding fell by 57 percent after the first two years of the program. In a year of bad drought and economic difficulties, serious and severe cases of malnutrition[f] dropped from a baseline of 19 percent to 12 percent, while they went up from 16 percent to 30 percent in areas used to compare results. A year later the net difference in serious and severe malnutrition, a midproject evaluation indicated, was over 40 percent among one- to three-year-olds. It declined by 23 percent in the pilot block (a subdivision of the Indian district; a block has about 100,000 people), while in the control it rose by 17.9 percent. Subsequent data showed that in all the districts where the program operated, the percentage of children who were normal or only mildly malnourished increased steadily. At the same time the percentage who were seriously or severely malnourished declined.

By late 1986 preliminary findings from the end-of-project evaluation pointed toward a 53 percent decline in serious and severe malnutrition, down to 8 percent of all children between seven months and five years old. Given what was happening to the economy during this period, there is fairly strong evidence that without TINP malnutrition rates would have been from 14 to at least 18 percent. (In the untreated area studied in 1986 serious and severe malnutrition was more than 20 percent.)

Most of those in TINP still classified as serious or severe cases were recent entrants to the program, which prompted project staff to reconsider the lower age limit of six months for program participation.

---

f. "Serious" and "severe" as used here in relation to the Tamil Nadu project refer to grades III and IV of the four-way classification of malnutrition used in India. (Some in India refer to both grades III and IV as "severe.") "Mild" and "moderate" malnutrition refer to grades I and II. Grade I is between 90 and 81 percent of median weight for age (based on standards issued by the Indian Council of Medical Research), grade II between 80 and 71, grade III between 70 and 61, and grade IV, 60 and below. A three-way so-called Gomez classification is used in most other countries, with grade I or "mild" malnutrition going from 90 to 76 percent of standard weight for age, grade II or "moderate" malnutrition from 75 to 61, and grade III or "severe" malnutrition, 60 and below. This is the system used in references here to projects in Brazil, Colombia, and Indonesia, although cutoff points sometimes vary by 1 percent.

Children under six months who were inadequately breastfed or prematurely weaned apparently were not being identified until their nutrition status was already seriously compromised.[g]

SUPPLEMENTATION IN BRAZIL. One component of the Brazil project provided supplementary feeding and preschool education to children four to six years old through the regular school system. Another instance of targeting by age and area (it concentrated on schools in poor locales), that program—PROAPE—was so well received in Brazilian communities that it is said to have opened the door for large-scale public preschool education throughout Brazil. Programs based on PROAPE have been set up in Colombia and Mexico, and several other Latin American countries are considering them.

A careful evaluation of CEAPE (a PROAPE counterpart program in São Paulo) found participating children fared better than others. With a daily supplementation of 250 to 300 calories (compared with 500 calories in PROAPE) and in far from ideal operating conditions, the shortfall from the norm in the heights and weights of participating children went from 52 percent to 46 percent at a time when the shortfall increased from 44 percent to 47 percent among nonparticipants. School performance scores for the following two years also were better and repetition rates lower among children who had been in the program.[6]

The measured impact of PROAPE itself on physical growth was only marginal, but evaluations showed that 73.5 percent of former PROAPE participants got passing grades in the first and second years of elementary school, compared with 59.5 percent in a group that did not participate. And the academic performance of children with two years' exposure to PROAPE was consistently better than that of the nonparticipating group, ranging from 2 to 21 percent in three variations of the model. Psychometric tests showed statistically significant improvement in PROAPE participants over a six-month period, though some of that was due to maturation.

OTHER FINDINGS. The targeted food programs shed light on a controversial issue in the nutrition field—the use of processed foods. Experience from the projects confirms that weaning food mixtures can be an important element in the success of supplementary feeding

g. The full impact of the project on infant and child mortality and morbidity, as well as project costs and effectiveness, are being assessed as part of two final evaluation studies, the reports of which are expected late in 1987.

programs and can promote nutritionally beneficial changes in behavior. Their development, however, must be based on careful study of food practices, local availability of inexpensive ingredients, and purchasing patterns of the target groups. Beyond weaning foods, special processed products (such as the enriched pastas provided in the Colombia project) are likely to have a greater nutrition impact than less expensive unprocessed foods only where there is clear evidence that malnutrition is mainly the result of imbalanced nutrient intake rather than the more common problem of low intake of everything.

The attraction of food as an incentive to encourage participation in other development activities was seen in both Brazil and Colombia. When food supplements used in a preschool stimulation program in Brazil were temporarily unavailable in some schools, participation declined 30 percent. In Colombia the availability of food coupons at health centers led to a marked increase in the utilization and effectiveness of the primary health care system.

One of the most important findings in the project experience is from the Rede Somar program in Brazil, which used geographic targeting to show that it was possible to reduce food prices for low-income families by increasing efficiencies in the food-marketing system. (This part of the Brazilian nutrition project, added late, replaced a component for development, testing, and production of low-cost, nutritious foods that for the most part never got under way.[h]) Under the Rede Somar program, a government food-marketing company attached to the Ministry of Agriculture sold certain basic foods to affiliated small and medium-size private retailers in low-income urban and rural areas who agreed to sell the products at specified prices. The retailers usually were allowed a 10 percent profit margin and were provided technical and operational assistance, including help with financing.

In general, COBAL (the marketing agency) reports, the consumer paid 20 to 25 percent less than normal market prices. The competition

h. The component that was to have promoted production of low-cost processed and fortified foods of high nutritional value was deleted from the project, largely because of differences between the government and the World Bank over subsidized interest rates on loans to the food industry. The intention had been that loans would be made to small and medium-size food companies and that, to reduce risk for the companies, the government would guarantee to take part of the production for use in public institutional feeding programs. One effort, although it involved considerable delay and heavy costs in getting under way, has developed and successfully tested a new method for processing cassava into flour. The method is sufficiently effective to have been replicated by forty cooperatives or small firms at their own expense.

that Rede Somar created among other food retailers in the Northeast, according to one study, reduced prices of basic food items by an average of 10 percent. Purchasing in bulk at lower prices by the agency to meet the needs of this financially self-sustaining program also lowered the cost of food obtained at the same time for other social programs. Economists have projected cost savings of 53 percent under this project and predict that even under highly adverse conditions its performance would be robust.[7]

Funding under the nutrition project allowed Rede Somar to expand to seven states in the Northeast, and the program was subsequently included in three other World Bank projects. The Brazilian government planned an even greater expansion of the program, and the government of Colombia, after studying Rede Somar, asked for and received Bank assistance in setting up a similar program.

The Colombia version of the program experimented with mobile markets as a means of increasing food consumption among the urban poor. Here the lesson learned was similar to that of the Brazil PINS program. Because these markets were offered only once or twice a week, they tended to benefit more those income groups who could afford to buy food for future days as well as the current day. The lower food prices in these markets, however, did benefit some poor groups as well, particularly in Cali, where 61 percent of the markets were located in low-income neighborhoods. To increase efficiencies and lower prices, the Colombia program also promoted and assisted small shopkeepers' associations, through which 577 merchants received training in marketing, as well as access to credit and warehouses.

Integrating Nutrition Assistance with Primary Health Care

The Colombia, India, and Indonesia projects all demonstrated the benefits of linking the delivery of health and nutrition services. Both the Indian and Indonesian projects required the establishment of a network of village-based workers. In Tamil Nadu the project operated through a linked system of village nutrition centers, each staffed by a locally recruited worker,[i] reinforced by health outreach and referral services.

i. Besides being from the village, the community nutrition worker (CNW) had to have completed the eighth standard at school (to be able to comprehend the written materials) and be considered a model mother of well-nourished children. Personality, ability

INDIA. The TINP community nutrition workers promoted the use of health facilities and, in turn, the health system provided supporting services to reinforce nutrition interventions. The program focused on growth monitoring and related nutrition education, treatment of diarrhea, deworming, immunization, and micronutrient (vitamin and mineral) and selective food supplementation. In addition to providing services to children, the program offered a number of the services—check-ups and referrals, tetanus immunizations, iron and folate tablets, and food supplements—to pregnant or lactating women.

The design of the nutrition delivery system drew heavily on experience with the training and visit system used in agricultural extension work. Workers were thoroughly trained to perform only a few critical tasks, the ratio of supervisors to workers was set realistically, and supervision was supportive, with an emphasis on in-service training to improve performance. Supervision was close and oriented toward encouragement and problem solving, rather than the fault-finding common in some supervisory situations.

Results from evaluations of both the pilot block and broader implementation of the Tamil Nadu project were extremely encouraging. The program was judged to be well organized and well administered. Workers knew their jobs and understood their priorities. They received frequent supervision and had adequate supplies for their work. As former Secretary of the Indian Planning Commission Asok Mitra reported, recruitment and training of the workers and supervisors for the program had been "quite thorough and will serve as models" to other government programs. "Each of the cadres," he wrote, "knew and performed their tasks well."[8] The major questions were whether the high quality of training, supervision, and administration could be sustained as the program expanded and whether the program would work in a state with less administrative capacity than Tamil Nadu.

By April 1983 trained community nutrition workers had been successfully installed in more than 4,000 community nutrition centers

---

to communicate, and the potential for leadership were considerations in her selection. She received sixty days of training and a modest remuneration of ninety rupees (about US $7.50) per month. The CNW was not a civil servant with specific office hours; instead she made herself available at times to suit the mothers. Thus, home visits were undertaken between 4 P.M. and 6 P.M., when mothers returned from work in the fields, while food supplementation was often carried out before 8 A.M. to enable mothers to complete on-site feedings before they went to work.

and by 1984 in over 9,000. For every ten workers there was one supervisor, which ensured visits at least twice a month to each center, allowed careful monitoring of record keeping, and helped maintain a high level of motivation. This was reflected in an impressively low turnover rate of under 2 percent.

In 1986 an assessment of the community nutrition workers by the United Nations Children's Fund (UNICEF) found that they still were "highly motivated, articulate and confident. . . . The degree of professionalism is unusual and impressive." The reviewers noted that the workers were widely known in their communities; most mothers and children could identify them. They were proud of the special recognition received in the village for their services. Their rapport with mothers, school children, teachers, and the multipurpose health workers was excellent.[9]

A rural health services component of the project provided for construction, furnishing, and equipping of 1,600 health subcenters, training of multipurpose health workers and health visitors, and construction of training facilities and training of instructors. In the first year of the program's implementation in the pilot block, coordination was poor between nutrition workers and supervisors, who come under the Social Welfare Department, and health workers and health visitors, who come under the Health Department. Prompt government action remedied that.

An evaluation in Madurai on program effects after four years revealed substantial improvements in health service coverage as a result of the project. Immunization coverage rose to 82 percent, as against 44 percent at the time of the baseline survey. Antenatal registration went from 39 to 70 percent, and coverage of tetanus toxoid injections for pregnant women increased from 23 to 62 percent.

Concerns have been raised that the considerable attention given to growth monitoring and the tight targeting—by way of stringent criteria of eligibility for food supplementation—in the Tamil Nadu project are too time-consuming and costly.[10] Some argue that a program that provides food for few children should be scrapped in favor of buying food for more children. But a principal goal of growth monitoring is to educate and support mothers in safeguarding and improving their children's nutrition. (And, indeed, the 1986 assessment found a strong awareness in the field staff that "their ultimate and all-important objective was to educate the mother and achieve appropriate changes in her behavior."[11]) By that measure screening can be a cost-effective device, particularly when back-up selective feeding is available for those who need it. The argument that an effort should be made to feed all children fails because such a program would be prohibitive in both cost and management requirements. And even though universal feeding might cover all of the needy, it would also reach many persons not threatened by malnutrition. Tamil Nadu's program, in fact, was *not* a conventional feeding program in scope, but one designed to minimize the need for food supplements by identifying faltering growth early on, before the child's nutrition status was seriously jeopardized. Fewer children, rather than more children, receiving the supplement was a positive indicator.

The entry requirement for food supplementation was two consecutive monthly readings of substandard growth, which, it has been argued, forecloses a rapid response to cases of acute malnutrition or rapid onset of growth failure. In practice, however, field staff exercised clinical judgment to ensure early intervention, and for children six to twelve months old, where rapid failure is more frequent, the observation period was reduced.

The close targeting of interventions on children under three years of age (based on the epidemiology of malnutrition in the area) proved efficient, for nutrition advantages derived from the program were shown to persist through sixty months of age. Children between ages four and five who had been through the program were a significant 1.75 kilograms (or 3.9 pounds) heavier than children from control villages. That the weight advantage was maintained two years after the children completed the program indicates the longer-run effects.

INDONESIA. In Indonesia, nutrition interventions at the village level have been regarded as the entry point for delivery of a broad range of health services. The World Bank assisted early in this effort through the Nutrition Intervention Pilot Project (NIPP), a field test of a range of community nutrition interventions (growth monitoring, oral rehydration therapy, nutrition education with emphasis on breastfeeding and weaning foods, home and village gardens to increase production of fruits and vegetables, and small-scale food processing and food storage, as well as immunization and, in selected areas, family planning counseling by traditional birth attendants). NIPP was set up with the intention of later integrating some combination of its services into a national nutrition strategy and program.

Nutrition and health services for children under the age of three and for pregnant and lactating women were to be offered in 180 villages of seven *kabupatens* (the major subdivision of provinces in Indonesia). The initial objective was to process locally grown foods and provide a nutritious product to those in need. Village volunteers (*kaders*) would monitor the growth of preschool children, distribute food to those who were not growing adequately, and provide nutrition education to their mothers. The program was expanded over four years and extended to 258 villages—43 percent more than planned. NIPP's short-term rehabilitative feeding concept was successful enough to be adopted for two other nutrition programs.

A study comparing the experience of children in the NIPP villages and those in the much larger but less intensive Indonesian National Family Nutrition Improvement Program (UPGK) found NIPP children started from lower nutrition status and reached the same levels as UPGK children by the end of the study period. NIPP children participated in the program to a greater extent, and there was greater change in their mothers' knowledge and behavior.[12] Another study showed that the proportion of children under three who were judged "well nourished" rose from 39 to 44 percent in one group of NIPP villages, but remained at 43 percent in comparison UPGK villages. In another group of NIPP villages, this figure rose from 36 to 46 percent, while in comparison UPGK villages it increased from 47 to 48 percent.[13] Within NIPP, some areas showed greater improvement than others; the better results appeared to be due to a more committed and active local leadership.[j]

A study of the Indonesian project demonstrated that village-level health services were likely to offer a more efficient and more equitable use of resources than comparable services offered higher up in the health system—at a subdistrict health center, for example.[14] A comparison showed that the cost per child of services provided through the village-level Nutrition Communication and Behavioral Change component of the project was 60 percent less than the cost of the same services at well-baby clinics at subdistrict health centers. Moreover, a substantially higher proportion of low-income people used the village services—73 percent of all low-income children participated in the

j. It is difficult to draw definitive conclusions about the impact of NIPP on levels of malnutrition in the target communities, in part *because* of all of these evaluations. Midproject evaluations led to significant modification in the program. Furthermore, some NIPP activities were spontaneously adopted in neighboring villages that were to have served as controls.

village program compared with less than 9 percent in the health center program.

COLOMBIA. In Colombia the food coupons distributed in the PAN program increased attendance at health centers, where preventive rather than curative care was emphasized, and locally recruited health workers (*promotoras*) and auxiliary nurses carried out nutrition surveys and delivered integrated health and nutrition services. The centers reached nearly 2 million people (half the total served in national primary health care), bringing many needy families into the orbit of the public health system.

The centers proved they could manage a food coupon system with few difficulties. (Clearly it was more manageable than direct food distribution, common in health centers elsewhere.) Integrating a food subsidy into the primary health care service helped people recognize that good nutrition, particularly of the target groups of young children and pregnant and nursing women, was essential to good health. Food coupons, in a sense, served as health center "prescriptions" to prevent and cure a "disease" known as malnutrition. A different tactic in Brazil, requiring a health check-up for eligibility in some locations in the subsidy program, was a failure; it caused participation to fall off so steeply that the requirement was dropped.

GENERAL FINDINGS. From all the projects it appears that nutrition interventions intended to benefit the poor will be more effective to the extent that they recognize the time and energy costs of participation and thus limit the number of changes they require in the normal habits of the benefiting population. Another lesson is that health and nutrition activities seem to be compatible, whether delivered by a community worker responsible for both or by separate health and nutrition workers, so long as tasks are well defined, cooperation is encouraged, and supplies of vaccines, drugs, nutrients, and food supplements are adequate and regular.

Linking Nutrition Assistance with Family Planning Objectives

A further important benefit of nutrition is its possible contribution to limiting fertility. Improved nutrition helps reduce infant and child deaths, which is thought to lessen the demand for more children: parents who realize that their children are likely to live to be adults may have fewer children and pay closer attention to their health and educational needs than parents who expect few offspring to survive.

Breastfeeding, a key element to good nutrition (its promotion is a common feature of most nutrition programs), plays a substantial role—through its suppression of ovarian activity—in influencing the length of the interval between births. For the 83 percent of couples in developing countries who, by estimates of the World Health Organization,[15] do not use modern forms of contraception, it is the principal determining factor of interval length.[k] Longer birth intervals usually mean that a woman will have fewer total births. The World Bank has estimated that, in the absence of breastfeeding, a woman in Bangladesh theoretically might have as many as six more births, in Indonesia five more, and in Senegal four more—the differences depend on the prevailing number of births per woman in each country and the relative contributions of other factors that determine fertility.[16]

Where the practice of breastfeeding has declined, the loss of contraceptive protection must be compensated by other factors, chiefly increasing use of modern contraception. Otherwise, fertility may actually increase, as it has in Kenya in recent decades. By one estimate the number of births in Sub-Saharan Africa would rise by 72 percent if breastfeeding and the sexual abstinence that frequently goes along with it no longer continued.[17] The need is to protect breastfeeding where it is still strong, as well as to promote it where it is declining.

All four projects included activities to promote breastfeeding. In Brazil, for instance, an explicit project objective was to extend the duration of breastfeeding among the rural poor, who are the least likely to be able to compensate for this resource after it is lost. Findings from a project-sponsored study on the use of commercial infant formula (a study that had impact beyond Brazil) contributed to the government's subsequent national breastfeeding campaign, to which UNICEF contributed financial and technical support.[18] In Colombia, a nine-month mass media campaign was conducted. Because health

k. At a world level it is estimated that in the mid-1970s lactational amenorrhea (the delay in resumption of menses after childbirth that is characteristic of women who breastfeed) in developing countries was providing approximately 38.5 million couple-years of protection, approximately 30 percent more protection against pregnancy than provided by the contraceptive methods of all the organized family planning programs in those countries. See Franz W. Rosa, "Breastfeeding in Family Planning," *PAG Bulletin*, vol. 5, no. 3 (1976), pp. 5–10.

personnel who are so influential in breastfeeding decisions are often themselves incompletely informed about breastfeeding, messages were aimed at them as well as the public. In addition to education messages, the campaign sponsored and achieved regulation of labeling, advertising, and promotion of infant formula, including bans on free samples to mothers in hospitals.

Delivery of nutrition services sometimes has led the way or helped to accelerate delivery of family planning services. Indonesia's family planning agency credits growth monitoring and related nutrition actions with having provided an important inducement for villagers to get together to discuss and become involved in family planning activities. Recent analysis showed a significant positive association between participation in nutrition program activities and use of intrauterine devices and oral contraceptives. A similar relationship was found between participation and length of the birth interval. Moreover, preliminary findings have shown current fertility, as measured by the percentage of women currently pregnant, to be inversely related to attendance in the nutrition program.[19] In the second Bank-assisted nutrition project with Indonesia, now in operation, nutrition at the village level is closely linked to family planning services.

In Tamil Nadu, family planning staff rely on community nutrition workers, who are based in the villages and have close contact with mothers, to identify villagers with unmet need for family planning. In a Bank-assisted population project in Thailand, nutrition has been used as the opening wedge to promote (as part of the national village rural poverty effort) an expanded primary health care system, which is itself an important element in the family planning program (see chapter 5). And the dramatic expansion of primary health care made possible under the Colombia nutrition project also helped expand family planning, which was among the services provided.

Changing Behavior through Nutrition Education

Nutrition education appears to be most effective when it is designed to modify specific behavior of specific groups of people with specific needs. In the Indonesian project, audiences of mothers with children under five were segmented by the age and health of the child, for instance—and messages were targeted to those in need of information at the time they needed it. These techniques were developed by working with intended audiences, understanding their attitudes, perceptions, and expectations, and encouraging them to try different actions and to formulate new ones to improve family nutrition.

The Nutrition Communication and Behavioral Change component in the Indonesian project was one of the first examples of what has become known as social marketing—the use of marketing techniques for social purposes, in this case, the marketing of improved nutrition practices. Although mass media and other marketing methods had been employed for some years to deliver messages about nutrition, few previous attempts had been made to do the kind of research and other efforts that are widely employed in commercial marketing to meet consumer needs.

Initially the project was to be implemented in sixty villages in five subdistricts, one of them a NIPP area. The first two years of the program were a preparatory phase, devoted to enlisting volunteer nutrition kaders and setting up a growth monitoring program. This infrastructure paralled that developed for the National Family Nutrition Improvement Program; the nutrition education effort was not established to create a new community nutrition project but rather to offer insights on the best communications strategy to produce improvements in nutrition status for the national program.

The third year was devoted to identifying the principal nutrition problems by group and taking the first steps to research, design, and test what eventually would be the messages to address these problems. A qualitative research program was designed to identify the beliefs, feelings, needs, constraints, and practices of mothers, with particular attention given to identifying those practices susceptible to change. Most of those interviewed were mothers of malnourished children. It was reasoned that, if these mothers could change their practices, so could most others. But mothers with well-nourished children (positive deviants) were also sought out to identify successful practices that were possible within the poor socioeconomic setting.

Solutions to the problems identified by the mothers had to promote family and community self-sufficiency, rather than dependence on outside resources. Households that included the mother of a malnourished child or a pregnant or lactating woman met individually with interviewers to agree on dietary modifications that the family then tried out. Resistances to adopting them were identified and became the focus of the education. The comments of the mothers in the interviews were analyzed as the study progressed, so that the question guides could be adapted to probe new hypotheses and ideas.

This trial step and the strategy design phase that followed helped the nutrition education team determine precisely what the program should aim to do (for example, introduce a homemade weaning food using locally available ingredients or change the preparation of oral rehydration solution—investigations showed that the practices advanced by existing national messages were inappropriate for the circumstances) and the best media and methods for doing it (for example, an innovative action poster for a mother to mark every time she performed a prescribed action or radio spots in dialogue format, using mothers' own words).

One year after the communication strategy went into operation, an evaluation showed that the 2,000 kaders had learned the program messages and that they had more specific advice to offer than kaders in other nutrition education programs in comparison areas; they were devoting on average nearly fourteen hours each month to nutrition work while volunteers in comparison areas gave fewer than seven hours. In project villages, 67 percent of households had been visited by a nutrition kader, in comparison villages 44 percent. Mothers in the project villages averaged 47 percent correct recall of nutrition messages, those in comparison villages 28 percent.

An evaluation of households confirmed changes in knowledge, practices, nutrient intake, and nutrition status of mothers and children in the project areas. Breastfeeding mothers and children in project areas ate a much greater variety and amount of the foods promoted by the program than did those in comparison villages.[20]

For children up to twenty-four months of age, mean weights for those in the program were from one-half to one kilogram higher than for those in comparison villages, a highly significant difference of at least half a standard deviation between mean weights. The growth curve for children in the program did not flatten until seven months of age, while the curve for comparison children flattened at five months. From seven months on, the lines were different but almost parallel. However, the average weight of the program children never fell below the normal zone, while the average for the comparison group dropped below normal starting at thirteen months of age. By the time children in the program reached the second half of their second year, 20 percent more of them had normal weight for their age than did the comparison children. Overall about 40 percent of those in the program exhibited better growth than those in the comparison group, and there were half as many moderately and severely malnourished children in the program group. These differences in nutrition status were seen not only across the entire sample but also in each geographic region. In each of five subdistricts analyzed, the nutrition status of program children was significantly better than that of comparison children.

Multiple regression analysis indicates that the difference in nutrition status can be attributed to the nutrition education program rather than to occupation, food expenditure, mother's age or education, radio ownership, or other factors. Women applied the knowledge gained in the program to feeding their children more of the recommended foods. In program areas, 87 percent of the children consumed more than half of the recommended calorie intake and 82 percent consumed more than half of the recommended protein intake; for children in the comparison sample, the figures were 62 and 60 percent, respectively. The most effective message was about a weaning food that is important to the nutrition status of infants five to eight months old, a crucial time in their development. A strong correlation was found between knowing about and preparing the food, indicating that the women not only learned but acted on the new knowledge.

The project appears to have been successful in finding a way around a frequent constraint to improved nutrition, the level of the mothers' formal education. This level is usually, as it was in the comparison group here, positively related to good nutrition status, suggesting that an important way to combat malnutrition is to increase schooling for girls. This route should certainly be pursued for its many obvious advantages—nutrition and otherwise. Still, nutrition messages that are clear and well targeted can be understood by women who have not had the benefit of much formal education. The less-schooled mothers who were exposed to the program's specific messages demonstrated nutrition knowledge as good as mothers with more formal education and their children had as good a nutrition status.

The communications component was the most successful of the Indonesian field programs. Its success was attributable to thorough marketing-type qualitative research, a carefully conceptualized media strategy, good implementation of the initial phase, and evaluation from the outset. The program had a demonstrably positive effect on the nutrition status of the target families—92 percent of whom could afford to do something (even if that meant only to feed their children an extra spoonful of rice), a condition amenable to behavioral change. The program provided only nutrition education, through a combination of personal contacts and messages in mass media. There was no supplemental feeding taking place in villages with the nutrition education program. Studies show that it was the *quality* of the education that made the difference.

Technical assistance was vital to the development of this component. One of the keys to success was the work of a nutrition anthropologist who lived in several project villages during most of the fourteen months of the program's formulation. She was able to determine, for example, that children were underweight, although breastfeeding practices appeared adequate. That children's growth began to falter early meant there was a problem. After many interviews and household observations, a team member discovered that women nursed with their left breast almost exclusively. A variety of explanations were given (for example, that mothers preferred to feed from the left breast for convenience because they could continue to work with their right hand), but the problem remained that children were not receiving the necessary quantity of breastmilk. The messages on breastfeeding were thus designed to encourage feeding from both breasts.

The program addressed only a few highly specific objectives. The messages were based on what people could and would do, and they were transmitted easily and effectively by village workers in home visits and weighing sessions, the latter offering opportunities for individual counseling with messages geared to the child's age and condition. These messages were reinforced by radio broadcasts. The program was successful because it built on the use of resources that already existed in the community. These principles for success would seem to apply regardless of a program's context.

In Tamil Nadu the communications program did not move smoothly. Delays in finding staff and in ironing out differences in approach toward nutrition education initially held up the mass media campaigns. Only one campaign, using radio broadcasts and printed material to teach better management of diarrhea, was undertaken during the first two years of the project. By the third year, however, the program was well under way. A large variety of materials was produced, including films that were required to be shown before the features at well-attended commercial movie houses. Building on the Tamil fascination with films, lyrics with nutrition education messages were adapted for singing with popular film tunes. Materials for training workers were also developed as part of the communications component, and the training part of the program functioned well throughout. Workshops held for nutrition staff before the project began were particularly useful.

The emphasis on monitoring of growth as a form of nutrition education (with short-term supplementary feeding as a corollary rather than dominant activity) paid off. The mothers' interpretation of growth lines on growth cards, according to the UNICEF assessment, was "accurate and impressive." Mothers were able to identify growth faltering, malnutrition, and a relapse with considerable skill and consistency. (Some 95 percent of mothers correctly interpreted normal growth, 89 percent understood poor nutrition status, and 85 percent appreciated the concept of growth faltering.) The assessment team found that mothers spontaneously used the card while explaining reasons for deviant growth, suggesting an effective use of the growth card by the community nutrition workers. The assessment concluded that the community nutrition workers possessed a remarkable degree of proficiency in all skills related to growth monitoring. The Tamil Nadu case demonstrated—as did the Indonesian nutrition education experience—that properly executed growth monitoring programs that stress the educational importance of the monitoring are feasible, acceptable to the community, and effective.[21]

The Colombia project undertook nutrition and health education, including mass media campaigns on specific problems. In these campaigns the techniques of message pretesting (trying messages out on a sample of people before going ahead with the campaign) were introduced in Colombia for the first time. Evaluation of the breastfeeding campaign indicated a significant change in attitudes toward breastfeeding among the target group of mothers with children under five years old.[22] (Resulting changes in actual practice and nutrition status were not examined.)

Brazil's experience in the PROAPE component of its project indicates that nutrition education for mothers in association with food programs and preschool education for their children can contribute to the improvement of nutrition and subsequent school performance.

Producing Food for Home Consumption and Income

Garden programs that were components of the nutrition projects in Colombia and Indonesia were successful in reaching the rural poor. Colombia's effort, designed to increase vegetable and small animal husbandry production and consumption among the poorest rural dwellers, was so popular it expanded into a small-scale rural development program for 45,700 households, more than double the planned estimates. It began as a modest effort to develop a technical package of seed, credit, and fertilizer suitable for home gardening and to train extension agents and rural teachers to demonstrate its use. The typical participant in the program grew food on a small plot (from half a hectare to five hectares of land) and worked for someone else. Many were small farmers outside the reach of previous credit schemes.

But the program in Colombia went so far beyond its original garden objectives—in the direction of small-scale farming—that its nutrition focus was diluted. An evaluation in 1982, when the new government ended the garden component, concluded that the program was responsible for 3,000 tons of production, that credit was the best-managed activity (89 percent of all recipients kept up on their payments), and that technical assistance and nutrition education activities needed strengthening. The impact on nutrition status was not evaluated.

The Indonesian home and village garden component offered extension services and grants for seeds, fertilizer, and other production-oriented inputs and services over a period of three years. Participating families, a 1982 evaluation found, spent more time working in their gardens, produced more, and grew a greater variety of vegetables than other families with gardens in their villages.[23] The majority of participants consumed about 60 percent of their vegetable production and attempted to market the rest. The great disappointment of the program was that it could not reach the families most in need of improved nutrition; the land available to them was just too small to make gardening practicable.

A second activity of the Indonesian program was to set up a model seed garden in each village through community efforts on communal land. Because of a lack of suitable land, the number of seed gardens established was well below that envisioned. But from even the limited experience it was seen that the concept was worth replicating. The

Ministry of Agriculture, which administered the program, is now actively promoting gardens as a regular part of its extension program.

As in Colombia's garden program, no attempt was made to look at the effect of Indonesia's garden program on the nutrition status of participating families. The closest approach to an evaluation of the nutrition impact of such small-scale food production programs occurred in a rural development project in Mauritius. There, 97 percent of the 2,300 families involved in a garden program claimed it had increased their food consumption and that their incomes had gone up 5 to 10 percent as a result of the sale of garden surplus.

Improvement of food production was a primary goal of the largest field component of the Brazilian project. This component, known by the Portuguese acronym PRAMENSE, sought to improve nutrition among 3,000 very low-income farm households in the state of Sergipe. It combined the work of agricultural and social (health and nutrition) extension agents with a new agricultural credit scheme (CAP) at a special low interest rate. Some combination of its services reached about 7,000 households, well beyond the initial goal.

Again, impact evaluation has been disappointing. In spite of an elaborate data collection and evaluation plan, no statistically significant evidence was collected on the direct impact of PRAMENSE on agricultural output, food consumption, or nutrition status. Reasons for the failure of the evaluation plan range from an overambitious research design to an inadequate baseline to the migration of control populations because of unprecedented drought. From the agricultural extensionists' point of view the program was a success: it increased the use of on-farm storage, improved seeds, animal traction for plowing, and, to a limited extent, chemical fertilizers.

Evaluation of PRAMENSE highlighted the importance of animal production in the survival strategies of small farmers and even sharecroppers. It also showed that in areas subject to frequent drought, crop insurance was needed to stimulate the purchase of modern inputs on credit. The CAP credit scheme managed to reach the lowest-income farmers and sharecroppers, who normally have no access to credit, and it was subsequently incorporated in Brazil's programs throughout the Northeast, including seven World Bank–assisted rural development projects. Local health associations formed under the project constructed thirty health posts, and this effort, too, along with other activities of the social extension workers, was made a standard part of the Bank's projects in the Northeast. A study of the experience under the PRAMENSE component highlighted the limitations in Brazil's Northeast of a rural development strategy that does not provide access to land for the rural landless.[24] The Bank later supported the decision to include the purchase and redistribution of land routinely in rural development projects in Brazil.

Improving Water and Sanitation

The Bank's experience with water and sanitation in nutrition projects is mostly limited to the Colombia project, in which it was the largest component financially, representing a quarter of project costs. The PAN program included an effort to increase access to potable water and improve environmental sanitation as a means of reducing the prevalence of diarrhea—a contributing cause of energy-protein malnutrition, particularly among children of preschool age—and other infectious diseases. By the end of 1984, some 427 water supply systems had been completed (the original target was 360); 35,000 latrines had been installed (the original target had been 112,000, revised down to 30,000 in 1980). The improved sanitation brought about by the installation of latrines and toilets had a clear effect. Evaluation data indicate that with every 10 percent increase in the number of households with latrines, the number of children with nutrition problems was reduced by 15 percent. (The impact of pit latrines was about half that of septic tanks and flushing toilets.)

By 1981, 40 percent of the half million rural dwellers in Colombia with access to piped water got it through the PAN program. In households that received piped drinking water, children's heights and weights were slightly greater than in other households, but it is not clear that the differences are statistically significant. (The lack of greater impact may be a reflection of the quality of the piped water.)[25]

Delivering Micronutrients

Iron and vitamin A supplements were provided in several of the programs. The largest effort was a program in Indonesia for prevention and control of anemia, designed to reach 10,000 workers on three government plantations and ten small private plantations. The program was based on research, undertaken jointly by the World Bank and the government of Indonesia, that had established that levels of nutritional anemia among adult male workers in Indonesia were ex-

tremely high and that substantial gains in productivity could be realized by treating this anemia.[26] The program's objective was to test
the feasibility of establishing a large-scale delivery system for iron
supplementation and to determine the economic effects of iron supplementation on output and employment.

The quick, successful development of the delivery system, plus
preliminary evidence of an increase in hemoglobin levels and productivity among workers, led to a fourfold increase in the program by the
end of 1981. In 1982, 300,000 workers were added to the program at
the expense of plantation owners. The 1982 evaluation of the Indonesia project gave cautious endorsement to the program, noting its
extension as evidence of the government's growing interest in nutritional anemia. However, a more careful evaluation of the impact on
health and productivity was urged before further expansion.[1]

Involving the Community

All four of the nutrition projects mobilized resources and volunteers in the community and went considerably beyond the standard
concepts of community participation, such as meetings to discuss
nutrition education. Local participation in the construction of health
posts and preschool facilities in Brazil and water sanitation facilities in
Colombia, in the formation of women's working groups in Tamil
Nadu, and in nutrition education through village nutrition workers in
Indonesia helped defray costs and improve the projects' quality. In
Colombia, for example, communities have borne, in the form of labor,
about half the cost of the construction of latrines and about 17 percent
of the installation costs of the water supply systems.

In the PROAPE program in Brazil, mothers regularly assisted teachers, thus contributing to the system's development and increasing
their own knowledge of nutrition. Fathers and other community
members donated time and materials to construct feeding and play
centers, reflecting their enthusiasm for the program. The high degree
of community participation has helped to lower costs and to
strengthen links between families and the local schools.

Moreover, efforts were also made to foster community-based orga-

1. The only more-thorough evaluation of a Bank-assisted micronutrient effort was in
the Philippines. There, in connection with a rainfed agricultural development project in
Ilo Ilo, iron deficiency anemia was 17 percent lower among women who received an
iron supplement.

nizations related to the programs. In Indonesia the NIPP program demonstrated the feasibility of a village-based nutrition rehabilitation effort, managed by community kaders supervised by health center staff and using a locally produced processed food to rehabilitate seriously malnourished children. Many neighboring communities that were not part of the NIPP program spontaneously organized themselves and raised the money necessary to establish similar programs in their own villages.

There are now some 9,000 women's working groups in Tamil Nadu, with an average in each of twenty-five women who meet twice a month at the homes of group members. The 1986 expert evaluation found that their "motivation is impressively high. The leadership quality is visible. Their skills in weighing and growth charting are considerable. Most can weigh correctly and fill growth cards. Their interpretation of growth lines is generally flawless. Their knowledge about infant feeding practices, diarrhea management, immunization, cause of deviant growth, and vitamin A deficiency is uniformly good."[27]

Each member "adopts" ten to fifteen families and assists the community nutrition worker in promoting their participation in the project and in seeing that children from these families are weighed, that messages are communicated to mothers, and so on. Over 200 of these groups produce weaning food for the program, some producing 800 kilograms a month. What each center produces beyond its own needs of 40 to 75 kilograms is distributed to other centers. Community nutrition workers believe that the women's working group is their most effective instrument. The credit for major improvement in mothers' understanding about feeding is essentially due to the performance of the women's working groups.

Generally, community participation generated enthusiasm in projects, raised awareness of nutrition, and improved the chances that project activities would continue after the projects ended. But there are costs as well as cost savings in a volunteer program. Part-time volunteers with limited skills take more time than regular workers to get a job done, there are more of them to be trained, tasks must be fewer and simpler, and quality control and supervision—key to successful community participation—are more difficult. Such costs, including the opportunity cost of the volunteers' time, must be taken into account when a volunteer system or other type of community involvement is part of the project. The three years' time required to work out details on the needs to be met in a community-based and community-identified nutrition project requested by the Senegalese government contributed to that project's eventually being dropped. The vastly different perceptions of priorities from community to community would have placed demands on so many government institutions that the project was seen by some officials as too complex to administer properly.

The range of opportunities for community participation varies from one culture to another. Many strategies assume that autonomous rural communities exist in some democratic form and can mobilize to manage their collective welfare in an egalitarian manner. For many traditional societies, these assumptions are just not valid. Other, less ambitious, models must be followed.

Local involvement—and beyond to local organizing and local management—is not only desirable; in some instances it is essential for the long-run success of nutrition activities. But, the planning of this important dimension must take account of the often severe constraints on what can be done at local levels, the financial limitations of local organizations, the length of time required to bring even small actions to fruition, the tenacity that must be exercised, and the variety of economic and other forces that lie beyond the control of local groups.

Building Institutions

Given the fragile base for dealing with nutrition in several of the project countries, a premium was put on institution building. This was best exemplified in the Indonesian project, where the principal objectives were to aid the government in the formulation and execution of a national food and nutrition program and to help build capacity to execute the program.

INDONESIA. The Indonesia project focused on strengthening and expanding staff and facilities of the Center for Research and Development in Nutrition (CRDN) and constructing, equipping, and staffing a new Food Technology Development Center (FTDC). The project also included programs for expanding and improving the training of nutritionists at the Academy of Nutrition and a new school for assistant nutritionists.

Strengthening the nutrition research center was a slow process, and its socioeconomic wing was never developed as envisioned, thus limiting its contribution to national planning. Nonetheless, the CRDN is now considered the best of Indonesia's five medical research institutes. Most of the government's training objectives for the center have been met, and evaluation skills are increasing.

The Food Technology Development Center is perhaps the first major facility in the world devoted largely to village-level food technology. A 1982 evaluation team was impressed with the quality of its leadership and its well-trained and highly motivated staff. Although construction problems slowed its work on food technologies, particularly on food storage, the FTDC succeeded in establishing machinery in the villages to produce the processed weaning food used in the NIPP component. (More recently, the FTDC has attracted funding from several other donors; its major project, financed by the Dutch government, deals with food safety.)

The Academy of Nutrition, whose facilities and staff were improved, is now regarded as one of the outstanding nutrition institutions in Asia and is attracting students from neighboring countries. The annual number of nutritionist graduates has increased from 60 to 200, and outside evaluators have praised the quality of their preparation. In 1985 the World Bank agreed to assist Indonesia in establishing two additional regional nutrition academies. Six new schools for assistant nutritionists also are to be established. A national staffing plan for nutrition, developed in the project to accompany the Fourth National Development Plan, is being implemented on schedule. The food and nutrition chapters of the development plan were the responsibility of an officer who completed his doctorate under the project and became head of nutrition and health services in the national planning agency.

Training has covered a broad range of skills and sophistication. For example, at the same time as some students were completing doctoral studies in nutrition planning, village kaders were learning about basic nutrition education. The project also funded 24 long-term fellowships and 180 short-course grants for technical specialists, training of kader supervisors, and training of nutritionists.

Building and strengthening these institutions required a sizable amount of external technical assistance, and the Indonesian institutions used it effectively. A large part of the assistance came from developing countries, particularly India and the Philippines, whose experience is relevant to Indonesia's needs. Four of every five of the consultants to the food technology institute, the nutrition academy, and the project secretariat were from developing countries, as were a third of those who aided the nutrition research institute.

In spite of shortcomings in evaluations, the continuing need for institution strengthening, and other (particularly management and coordination) problems, the Indonesian government has established a strong base in a remarkably short period. A team of international and Indonesian nutrition experts in 1982 credited the project with "strengthening and expanding the infrastructure for a larger-scale nutrition program" in Indonesia and noted the "quite impressive" effect of its action programs.[28]

Efforts by UNICEF and the U.S. Agency for International Development, in addition to the Bank project, have contributed, directly and indirectly, to the nutrition program in Indonesia. Nutrition now plays so large a role in Indonesia (including its function as an entry point for family planning and women's development activities) that it is frequently referred to as a movement, with few parallels elsewhere.

BRAZIL. In the Brazil project, the National Food and Nutrition Institute (INAN) was responsible for staff training, technical assistance, and support for evaluation of the project components and other special studies. The objective was to enhance INAN's management capability. Unfortunately, INAN's lack of prestige within the government or the nutrition community, as reflected in part in its failure to be raised to the status of a foundation, was a limiting factor that made it difficult for INAN to attract highly qualified nutritionists and economists. Nevertheless, credit for development of the nation's large nutrition program must go to INAN.

The project was to establish a unit in the Brazilian Institute of Geography and Statistics to undertake a national nutrition survey and to update it periodically. This was to be in follow-up to a survey that had gathered extensive socioeconomic, demographic, food consumption, and anthropometric data on 55,000 families. Political sensitivity to the findings of the earlier survey (for example, approximately 50 percent of urban families and 43 percent of rural families in the Northeast had been found to receive less than 90 percent of what was considered necessary food energy) kept the follow-up survey from taking place. However, the data from the earlier survey were studied by a special unit funded by the project within the research management agency, FINEP, which reports to Brazil's Secretariat of Planning. Eventually, the government established an ongoing policy-oriented nutrition research program jointly administered by FINEP, INAN, and the National Science Council.

An encouraging aspect of Brazil's project has been a large gain in the number of people and institutions equipped to deal with nutrition problems. Nutrition services are being provided by 250,000 preschool teachers. An evaluation of the project reported that "top flight agricultural planners, economists and other social scientists, sparked by project funds, are devoting substantial portions of their careers to nutrition-related topics. And this is reflected in the programs of their institutions."[29]

COLOMBIA. In Colombia, one of the nutrition project's achievements was to strengthen the primary health care system through the building or renovating of 729 health care posts, more than double the initial estimate, and through the development of sound plans for continued expansion of coverage under a subsequent World Bank health loan. Nutrition services not previously available are now being provided, as a result of the nutrition project, through 3,500 newly recruited and trained primary health care workers. A graduate program in nutrition was established at Javeriana University. The project also supported work by the Institute of Technological Research to develop a quality control system for food, stimulate investment in commercial processing of nutritious foods, develop small-scale portable food-processing equipment, and improve methods of on-farm storage. By 1985 the institute had completed forty-three studies on a range of food-processing and packaging improvements. The same institute, collaborating with the Colombian National Institute of Health, established a national network of nine regional quality control laboratories and a national quality control system that is functioning reasonably smoothly. Because of project activities, the National Institute of Health also is better equipped, more extensive, and more capable in constructing water systems.

A major institution-building goal in Colombia's project was development of a strong coordinating group for nutrition in the National Planning Department. It would have the capacity to organize and evaluate nutrition projects and create a permanent focus for the consideration of nutrition concerns that transcends the responsibilities of particular ministries. The project did help to strengthen the managerial capacity for planning and executing the nutrition program and stimulated progress toward regional planning and administration.

Much of the momentum, however, was lost when a new government came to power and assigned a lesser priority to nutrition and the PAN program.

INDIA. The project in Tamil Nadu was developed within an administrative structure that was already strong. Institution building there consisted of creating links between the health and social welfare departments, links that now are strong and well established. The project set up the infrastructure for delivery of nutrition services by recruiting, training, and deploying a community nutrition worker in each of 9,000 communities, as well as the instructors, supervisors, and nutrition officers who support this system.

An unusually strong training program was the key to the success of the project and its possibilities for long-term effects. Training in village-level programs elsewhere generally ranges from a few days to a week. Workers at all levels in Tamil Nadu received about two months of training, with stress on reinforcement through in-service training. More than one-third of that was practical field training. Questions were raised at the outset about the high cost of such extensive training compared with other programs, but the investment appears to have paid off.

The Tamil Nadu project also was responsible for establishing nutrition centers in each of the communities (mostly by renting and renovating existing facilities) and for constructing a health subcenter for about every five communities, or 1,600 subcenters in all. At the state level, a powerful communications unit was established, which the state government intends to expand into a communications center to serve other social welfare and health activities.

OTHER OUTCOMES. The least successful element of the institution-building strategy in the nutrition projects, except in Tamil Nadu, was the strengthening of entities responsible for directing or coordinating nutrition activities. The widespread problems of weak organizations in social sectors and the inherent difficulties of improving internal organization, procedures, and staff, along with the demands on institutions to take on new roles and responsibilities, clearly made management more difficult and time-consuming than had been anticipated.

Personnel shifts are an important, seldom reported part of institution building. In two countries, top-level changes made in conjunction with managing the projects led to marked improvements that were felt well beyond the projects.

The nutrition projects have also helped strengthen nutrition communities. The projects have played a catalytic role in providing opportunities and a rallying point for existing nutrition activities. New groups, including those in disciplines not previously involved with nutrition, have been given reason to address nutrition issues and now form part of the nutrition constituencies of their countries.

3 | Costs, Affordability, and Cost-Effectiveness

THE ANNUAL COSTS of activities related to the four nutrition projects varied widely because of differences in the size of the projects, the extent of targeting, the amount of food provided, and the prevailing levels of wages, food prices, and food consumption. Costs covered by World Bank and government sources ranged from $146,000 a year for the initiation phase of the nutrition education component of the Indonesia project, which entailed no food distribution, to more than $8 million a year for the Tamil Nadu comprehensive nutrition and health services component at full program height, when upwards of one million women and children were benefiting from a range of services.

Comparing Costs

Table 3-1 compares annual costs overall and for each beneficiary. It also compares costs for serving a group of 100,000 people and for transferring 1,000 calories. Because of the different types of projects, their different aims and different outcomes, cross-project comparisons with the data are not always appropriate. And because of national differences, the costs of a project in one country would not necessarily be replicable in another. Furthermore, the quality of the data, while quite good for projects of this type, is uneven.

In annual costs per beneficiary, the least expensive by far was the Indonesia nutrition education program, initially at $4 and projected to decline during expansion to $2, because no food transfers were involved and much of the fieldwork was done by volunteers. At the other end of the scale were the highly intensive NIPP in Indonesia at $56 and Brazil's preschool feeding and stimulation program (PROAPE) at $47. The Colombian and Brazilian food subsidy programs for con-

46

sumers, at $35 and $21, respectively, differed in cost partly because of the larger number of health and nutrition services in the Colombian program. In Tamil Nadu, costs per beneficiary can be viewed in more than one way, because different types of services were available. The overall cost per beneficiary for the comprehensive nutrition and health services was $9, and beneficiaries received one or more of a number of health and nutrition services. The largest part of all component costs belonged to the weighing, nutrition education, and feeding portion, where the average cost per beneficiary was $12. The cost per child weighed and screened (and whose mother received nutrition education) was $7.

The cost per beneficiary, however, does not reflect the volume and quality of services provided or improvements brought about by the program. In Tamil Nadu the cost per child in the program fell 19 percent between 1982 and 1985, as fewer children required the rehabilitative feeding. Furthermore, the cost per beneficiary, like the other measures in table 3-1, includes only the direct public sector cost of the program. It does not capture the costs of transportation and time spent by the beneficiary in using the service, the purchase price of subsidized foods, and the additional food that an education program convinces people they should buy.

Costs are compared for populations of 100,000 (the total population from which beneficiaries are drawn), and constant returns to scale are assumed. Food subsidies initiated in Brazil and Colombia cost $399,000 and $438,000, respectively, per group of 100,000 persons, while the weighing and selective feeding programs in Indonesia and India cost $98,000 and $102,000, or about $1 per capita. The differences reflect primarily the size of the target group within the total population, the effectiveness of the coverage of that group, the length of time people were fed, the amount of food and other services per beneficiary, and country cost factors.

In Brazil, entire families were fed; in Colombia, children under five and pregnant and nursing women; in NIPP in Indonesia, children under three with existing or potential signs of malnutrition and malnourished pregnant and nursing women; and in India, children from six months to three years old who were not growing adequately (and who were released when their nutrition status improved) and mothers in need. Since the Indian and Indonesian programs were much more selective, overall food costs were kept to a minimum. Moreover, proportionately fewer children require feeding as programs begin to

Table 3-1. Annual Costs of Some Components in Four World Bank–Supported Nutrition Projects

Project, component, and year	Overall cost (thousands of dollars)				Population served (thousands)	Number of beneficiaries (thousands)	Cost per beneficiary (dollars)	Cost to deliver 1,000 calories (dollars)	Cost per 100,000 persons (thousands of dollars)			
	Non-recurrent[a]	Recurrent		Total					Non-recurrent	Recurrent		Total
		Food	Other							Food	Other	
Brazil												
Food subsidy (PINS), 1980	(.)	723	152	875	219[b]	41	21.34	0.30[c]	(.)	330	69	399
Preschool feeding and education (PROAPE), 1980	7	435	594	1,036	—	22	47.09	0.53[d]	—	—	—	—
Colombia												
Food subsidy, 1981	—	2,653	1,551[e]	4,204[f]	960	120	35.03	0.79[g]	—	276	162[e]	438
India												
Comprehensive nutrition and health services, Tamil Nadu, 1984–85[h]	—	2,491	5,984	8,475	8,250	900	9.41	0.69[i]	—	30	72	102
Weighing and feeding portion[j]	(.)	2,491	3,161	5,652	8,250	484[k]	11.67[l]	0.69	—	—	—	—
Indonesia												
Weighing and feeding program (NIPP, Bojonegoro area), 1982	388	77	74	539	194	—	—	—	20	40	38	98
Weighing and screening	—	—	—	—	—	15	12.74	—	—	—	—	—
Feeding	—	—	—	—	—	2	56.01	—	—	—	—	—

Nutrition education, 1977–81											
Initiation phase[m]	83	—	63	146	225	37	3.94	—	37	—	28	65
Expansion phase[n]	36	—	40	76	225	37	2.05	—	16	—	18	34

(.) Negligible.

Note: Costs are financial costs. Some figures have been rounded. Dashes indicate information is unavailable or inapplicable.

a. Annualized for the project component periods, which vary from three to five years. For India, costs are for the most recent year available.

b. Estimate derived by tripling the 10,000 families having two minimum salaries or less targeted for the subsidy program, since a third of families in the project area fall in that category, then multiplying by 7.3, the average family size in the lowest income group in urban Northeast Brazil.

c. Based on 600 calories a person a day at 50 percent subsidy for 27,000 recipients for the full year (some of the 41,026 beneficiaries participated for less than a full year).

d. Based on 500 calories a person a day at 100 percent subsidy for 14,055 children for 217 days, 4,270 for 131 days, and 3,973 for 60 days.

e. No information is available on nonrecurrent costs for 1981 or previous year; other recurrent costs may include some training costs, which are nonrecurrent costs.

f. The full cost of the subsidy borne by the Colombian government; costs of evaluating the effectiveness of the program were financed by the project.

g. Based on 5,227 tons of food, the value of coupons redeemed.

h. Includes diarrhea management, deworming, immunization, folic acid treatment, and other services, as well as weighing and feeding. Costs are for April 1, 1984–March 31, 1985.

i. Based on costs of food, staff time, transportation, equipment, and training.

j. Includes nutrition education.

k. Represents 450,000 children weighed (120,000, or 27 percent, of whom were also fed) and 34,000 mothers who were fed.

l. The beneficiary cost can be conveyed in other ways as well. The cost per child weighed and screened was $7.02 (mothers of these children also received nutrition education). For the 154,000 children and mothers who required feeding, the food cost per recipient was $16.17.

m. Includes one-time fixed costs, such as research, message development, and materials design.

n. Excludes fixed costs.

Source: For detailed component costs of projects in Brazil, Colombia, and Indonesia: T. J. Ho, "Economic Issues: Costs, Affordability, and Cost-Effectiveness," World Bank, Population, Health, and Nutrition Department, Washington, D.C., 1983. For costs in India: data from a cost analysis conducted by David Dapice for the World Bank in late 1986.

improve the nutrition status of participants; annual food costs in the Indian pilot block began at $43,000 and have declined to $16,800 as the number of malnourished children declined. And because less food was required for the more narrowly targeted programs, the administrative, delivery, and other recurrent costs for food were kept lower, even though screening imposed additional costs. Nonfood recurrent costs were a higher proportion of costs in highly targeted direct feeding programs (as in Tamil Nadu) than in more generalized food subsidy programs (as in Brazil). The need to weigh children monthly required more contact with beneficiaries, but it also provided the opportunity to include nutrition education and primary health care for the children and to spread costs commensurately. Nonfood recurrent costs also were a higher proportion of the Colombian subsidy program, which required participants to collect food coupons at health facilities, although that requirement led to benefits in the form of other nutrition and health services as well.

Nutrition education as implemented in Indonesia was the least expensive of the components per population of 100,000, at $65,000 annually during initiation and an estimated $34,000 during expansion. Again, this low level of costs is expected since no food transfers were involved. Expenditures during the initiation phase were much higher than during the expansion phase mainly because the developmental research and other elements in the design and testing of messages are expensive initial costs that need not be repeated during expansion.

The cost of delivering 1,000 calories, as shown in table 3-1, rose with the degree of targeting—from $0.30 for the Brazil subsidy program to $0.53 for Brazil's more closely targeted preschool program, to $0.69 for Tamil Nadu's feeding program, the most tightly targeted of the efforts. The Colombian subsidy program at $0.79 was the highest, partly because of the nonfood services included, but also because of the use of more expensive processed foods.

Generally, the cost per beneficiary in all the Bank-assisted programs compares favorably with feeding programs in other countries, which range from $11 to more than $200.[1] In Brazil, for example, PROAPE at $47 per beneficiary costs significantly less than three other preschool feeding programs in the state of Alagoas—about half the cost in one case and less than a third the cost in the two others— largely because PROAPE relied on support from mothers and others in the community, did not need elaborate kitchens and running water, and used lower-cost foods.

Affordability

Would interventions be affordable for governments if the projects were extended nationwide? The answer depends on a number of factors, not the least being the importance a government assigns to the malnutrition problem and its willingness to commit resources in this area. Clearly, an intervention such as Brazil's Rede Somar food marketing program is affordable, inasmuch as it is self-supporting. Similarly, a program such as Indonesia's anemia effort, in which costs could largely be borne by employers who receive substantial production benefits, does not present serious financial problems.

Table 3-2 shows the cost of expanding other programs nationwide, with those costs expressed as percentages of the national budgets for the years indicated.[a] These rough estimates, which assume that the costs per beneficiary observed in smaller programs would continue in larger ones, may in fact underestimate costs (because additional groups may be harder to reach and less eager to accept the services) or overestimate them (because of economies of scale). For many countries the expansions could be financed out of current expenditures for nutrition, if those expenditures were restructured to make more efficient use of resources.[b]

Many low-income countries now spend 6 percent or less of their budgets on health and nutrition. Some, however, devote substantial portions of their budgets to consumer food subsidies, but generally do not perceive or budget them as nutrition programs. In 1975 food subsidies accounted for 21 percent of Egypt's total government expenditures, 19 percent of Korea's, 16 percent of Sri Lanka's, and 12

a. In Colombia expansion refers to all designated poverty areas only.
b. Portions of some programs can also be borne by the consumer or covered through cross subsidies. A means of limiting the costs the poor incur has been tested in India, where the government for a period required nutrient fortification of *atta*, the processed form of wheat used to make the *chappati*, the staple of the North Indian diet. Through its price controls, the government encouraged the miller to spread the fortifying costs to consumers of all processed wheat products; upper-income groups, who consumed mostly refined wheat flours, carried much of the expense while the fortified atta cost the beneficiaries less than they would otherwise have paid.

Table 3-2. Annual Projected Recurrent Costs of Nutrition Programs
Expanded to Entire Country and Their Share of National Budget

Project, component, and year	Population served by expansion (thousands)[a]	Cost per 100,000 persons (thousands of dollars)[b]	Cost of expanded coverage (millions of dollars)	National budget (millions of dollars)	Cost of expanded coverage as percentage of national budget
Brazil					
Food subsidy (PINS), 1980	118,332	399	472	18,183	2.60
PINS for urban areas only, 1980	66,685	399	266	18,183	1.46
Colombia[c]					
Food subsidy, 1981	7,928	438	35	1,807	1.94
India					
Comprehensive nutrition and health services, 1984	750,000	102	765	35,968	2.12
Indonesia					
NIPP, 1982	122,722	78	96	25,052	0.38
Nutrition education, expansion phase, 1981	120,507	28	34	22,002	0.15

a. Total national population, except for Colombia, which is 30 percent of total population.
b. From table 3-1.
c. Expansion to all designated poverty areas in country (30 percent of total population).
Source: World Bank data.

percent of Morocco's. In 1981 the urban food subsidy in China accounted for 13 percent of government expenditures. Although for many countries these levels have proved too high to sustain, the examples suggest how substantial the commitments can sometimes be.

If neither a reallocation of existing resources nor some form of cost recovery were possible, costs for the actions taken under the four nutrition projects would range from 0.15 to 2.6 percent of national budgets. Indonesia's NIPP, for example, would cost 0.38 percent of the national budget and its nutrition education program 0.15 percent (see table 3-2). Colombia's food subsidy program would be considerably higher at 1.94 percent, and Brazil's, at 2.6 percent, would be higher still. The cost of Brazil's program, if it were directed to the urban poor only, as it probably would be, would fall to about 1.46 percent. Even if it were not limited to the urban poor, a nationwide program would actually cost less than the projected 2.6 percent of the national budget, since the calculations are based on the distribution of the poor in the Northeast and there are relatively fewer poor in most of the country. The cost would be less if the project were restricted to the poor in the lowest-income regions of the country, as was the case in Colombia, where the design was to reach 30 percent of the population through geographic targeting. India's comprehensive nutrition and health delivery component, at 2.12 percent of the national budget, falls in the middle range.

Measuring Benefits

Considerable attention has been given to attempting to measure the effects of the four nutrition projects. It would be desirable to have complete information on all the effects, but information of this sort is never obtained comprehensively in operational settings, and in the four nutrition projects more has been gathered in some areas than in others. Quite good information that deals with process—output rather than impact—has been collected for most of the Bank-assisted project components. For several, project data are available on the impact of certain components that can be used in analyzing cost-effectiveness. Fortunately, too, other World Bank research during the same period has provided data, especially on the relation of nutrition to the potential for increased productivity and educability, that can be used to judge what might be expected from nutrition interventions.

Cost-Effectiveness

The Tamil Nadu Integrated Nutrition Project (TINP) can be compared with that state's segment of the nationwide Integrated Child Development Scheme (ICDS). Annual direct costs (mostly food and salaries) for each community nutrition center under that project are $579, against nearly double that, $1,129, for comparable services at each ICDS center. (When health service costs and training and supervision costs other than salaries are included, costs of the Tamil Nadu project rise, but figures for comparison are not available for ICDS.

Neither are indirect costs available, such as the cost of volunteers' time.)

ICDS centers cover about 10–20 percent fewer people than do centers under TINP. On average, the ICDS program weighs fewer children per post (forty-three compared with sixty), but feeds relatively more of them at any given time (100 percent against 27 percent for the Tamil Nadu project) since everyone who is weighed is fed.

Despite the lower direct costs, primarily the result of proportionately fewer children being eligible for feeding, the Tamil Nadu project appears to have had greater impact on nutrition status among children six to thirty-six months of age: serious and severe malnutrition has declined by 30 to 50 percent, while in the ICDS areas the decline has been between 10 and 20 percent. Thus, it appears that the Tamil Nadu project, even if it were to prove comparable in total direct costs, may have had two to three times the impact on malnutrition as the ICDS project.[2]

In Indonesia, the nutrition status of children up to twenty-four months old in five areas covered by the nutrition education component of the project can be compared with that in five areas covered by different programs of nutrition education and other nutrition activities from other major government programs, including NIPP. One year after the full implementation of the communications strategy, significant differences emerged between project and comparison villages in the percentage of malnourished children, as measured by shortfalls from the standard weight for the children's age group:

Percentage of standard weight-for-age	Children in nutrition education villages	Children in comparison villages
Less than 60	0.0	1.2
60–74	10.0	18.2
75–89	42.4	40.0
90 or more	47.6	40.6

There were no significant differences between villages before the program, and no other factors were found to explain the improvements. The NIPP component cost $97,760 annually to cover a population of 100,000, and the nutrition education component cost $65,180 (and was projected to decline to $33,990 once it was fully operational). If the NIPP outcomes are assumed to be the same as outcomes overall in comparison villages, the nutrition education component is more cost-effective than NIPP, producing a greater impact at a lower cost. Similarly, in another program taking place in some of the comparison villages, the National Family Nutrition Improvement Program, costs to cover the same size population, at $91,075, were higher than the cost of the nutrition education component (and were higher still when supplementary feeding is included). This difference again suggests that the approaches employed in the nutrition education component were more cost-effective.

Reductions in Morbidity and Mortality

If the Tamil Nadu project were implemented statewide at the level of quality it had in early 1983, projected estimates suggest that about 107,000 fewer children might suffer serious or severe malnutrition than might otherwise be expected. Over a four-year period 76,000 fewer might suffer moderate malnutrition, and 12,385 fewer might die.[c] But that figure excludes children less than six months old (because they were not part of the original target group, they were not counted in the baseline survey) and those three to five years old (because death rates for that group are not available).[3] Thus the estimate of total deaths that might be averted is low, and any cost estimate per death averted would be high.

In this analysis conducted by T. J. Ho, the projected annual cost of overcoming malnutrition through a statewide expansion of the Tamil Nadu project would range from $33 to $126 a child, depending on the severity of the case.[4] The Tamil Nadu costs have the potential to be strikingly lower than those of well-documented, traditional nutrition rehabilitation programs: in Haiti the cost of improving children's weight was estimated at $600 a child, and the cost of eliminating severe malnutrition at $3,600 a child; in Guatemala the cost for the latter was an estimated $5,300 a child.[5] Although preventing deaths is not necessarily the principal objective of nutrition programs, the costs of the Tamil Nadu project would also be within the range, albeit the higher end of the range, of more conventional health approaches to

c. Calculations about deaths averted are based on a probability index showing the number of children six to thirty-six months old that can be expected to die in the Punjab and on a reasonable set of assumptions about external influences. See A. A. Kielmann and Colin McCord, "Weight for Age as an Index of Risk of Death in Children," *Lancet*, vol. 1, no. 8076 (June 10, 1978), pp. 1247–50.

reducing mortality. The cost per death averted in a statewide Tamil Nadu program is projected to be $1,482 a year. This figure is generally lower than the cost per death prevented through malaria control, polio immunization, community water supply and sanitation projects, and hospital care, but higher than the costs of immunization against measles, tetanus, and typhoid.

Nutrition programs also reduce illness, improve growth in later childhood, and enhance the quality of life as malnutrition is overcome (see table 3-3). The demonstrated relationships between malnutrition and the capacity for increased productivity and learning indicate further benefits from better nutrition. Even within the narrow context of mortality control, nutrition interventions aimed at children less than three years old are likely not only to reduce the mortality of those children but also to reduce subsequent births to their parents, making nutrition a possible fertility reduction intervention.

Table 3-3. Expected Principal Benefits of Interventions
That Increase Food and Nutrient Intake of Children and Adults

Beneficiary	Improved physical development	Improved mental development[a]	Increased capacity to work[b]	Reduced severity and duration of disease	Reduced malnutrition	Reduced infant and child mortality
Child						
Preschool, 0–3 years	x	x	—	x	x	x
Preschool, 4–6 years	x	x	—	x	x	—
School-age, in school	x	x	—	x	x	—
School-age, out of school	x	—	x	x	x	—
Adult						
Male	—	—	x	x	x	—
Female, pregnant or lactating	—	—	x	x	x	x
Female, non-pregnant and nonlactating	—	—	x	x	x	—

x Expected.
— In some cases where this mark is shown, less dramatic but still positive benefits are likely to accrue to beneficiaries (for example, physical development of adults); in other cases, benefits are not applicable to some groups.
a. Resulting from increased activity and mental alertness.
b. Refers to increases in current capacity only.
Source: Ho, "Economic Issues."

The cost of preventing blindness caused by vitamin A deficiency has not been computed for the Bank-assisted projects (three included distribution of vitamin A), but the cost of preventing blindness in a successful program that distributed vitamin A in Bangladesh is estimated at about $350 per case averted (in addition, vitamin A provides greater resistance to infection and other benefits). This compares with an estimated $6,700 to prevent a case of blindness in the Onchocerciasis Control Program, which also provides other benefits.[6]

Cognitive Development and School Performance

In Brazil the principal benefit sought in the PROAPE program, combining nutrition and education activities for preschoolers, was an improvement in cognitive development and subsequent school performance. Of the children who had been in PROAPE, 93 percent in a sample group completed the first year of school and 68 percent of that group passed to the second; in the second grade 94 percent of the remaining children completed the year and 79 percent of these passed. Non PROAPE children did less well (see table 3-4). The total cost of schooling (including preschool PROAPE services) per second-grade graduate was about $50 (or 11 percent) less for students who had been in the PROAPE program than for those who had not been in PROAPE. On the basis of these results, a strategy that combines investment in PROAPE with schooling appears to be more cost-effective than investment in schooling alone.

IN SHORT, compared with earlier interventions (which generally were either indiscriminate in their coverage or, if targeted, involved one-on-one treatment and oversight from highly trained professionals), the large-scale concepts tried in the Bank-assisted projects appear to have shown the feasibility of pushing per capita beneficiary costs down to relatively low levels. In some instances the costs of these efforts could be met by restructuring existing programs. Even if the costs were added in full to the government budget, most of the interventions appear to be affordable if extended on a much wider scale.

The low-cost nutrition education as practiced in Indonesia looks particularly attractive. The cost per child of improving nutrition status was estimated at $9.85 a year during the pilot phase and $5.15 a year for an expanded program. That it was cheaper than programs requir-

Table 3-4. Cost-Effectiveness of PROAPE Preschool Feeding and
Stimulation Program in Brazil

Measure	PROAPE	Non-PROAPE
Number of first-grade entrants	22,298	22,298
Dropout rate (percent)		
First grade	7	9
Second grade	6	6
Repeater rate (percent)[a]		
First grade	32	43
Second grade	21	38
Graduation rate (percent)[b]		
First grade	63	52
Second grade	74	58
Number of graduates		
First grade	14,048	11,595
Second grade	10,396	6,725
Cost (dollars)		
Project cost	1,036,370	—
First-grade education[c]	2,185,200	2,185,200
Second-grade education[d]	1,376,700	1,136,310
Total	4,596,270	3,321,510
Cost per second-grade graduate	442	494

— Not applicable.
a. Percentage of nondropouts failing to pass to the next grade.
b. Percentage of total entrants to the grade passing to the next grade.
c. Estimate based on the annual cost per primary student in Nicaragua ($98), on which data were available, times the number of first-grade entrants in the sample (22,298). First-grade repeaters are excluded. The estimate assumes that the cost and efficiency of the educational systems in Nicaragua and Northeast Brazil were comparable at the time of the program.
d. Estimate based on the assumed annual cost per primary student ($98) times the number of first-grade graduates.
Source: Vital Didonet, "Atendimento integrado de educação saúde nutrição, e envolvimento comunitario do pre-escolar, através de metodologia de baixo custo e ampla cobertura: síntese da exposição," paper presented at the World Assembly of Preschool Education, Quebec, August 28–September 2, 1980; education costs derived from data of the Nicaragua Academy for Educational Development, 1975.

ing food commodities comes as no surprise; the question is whether it was effective. The evidence has shown that nutrition education alone *can* make a difference in improving nutrition status. Nutritionists have long held out the promise of this possibility; the Indonesian experience is the first time it has been demonstrated in an operational setting.

Even though it is at the high end of the cost spectrum, a consumer food subsidy program that is properly targeted can be affordable in certain contexts. And in countries that are trying to achieve a more equitable distribution of income, but for whom cash transfers are politically unacceptable, the targeted consumer food subsidy may be a financially feasible and politically viable means of working toward that end. (Apart from whatever income is transferred in such a program is the question of whether it increases food consumption. In the Colombia project, the only one in which this question was examined, consumption does appear to have increased.)

Among other project efforts, vitamin A programs clearly are cost-effective. Brazil's preschool feeding and stimulation program is a relatively costly nutrition intervention, but it may be a less costly way to strengthen an education system than other conventional approaches, such as building more schools. The Tamil Nadu approach to preventing deaths is more costly than some and less costly than other common approaches; the other benefits of that program, however, go well beyond most health approaches.

Finally, through this accumulated project experience and the concurrent research undertaken by the Bank, a good deal has been learned about nutrition economics, although much remains to be learned. The economic analysis employed in conjunction with these projects has identified useful areas that merit exploration in future cost analysis in this relatively new field.

4 | Questions of Design

ALTHOUGH PROGRESS was made, the initial three nutrition projects that the World Bank helped to set up in the late 1970s were so complex in design that they were administratively cumbersome. They tried to do too many things and to test too many approaches; they sometimes expanded too rapidly; and they optimistically assumed a higher degree of management skill and organizational capacity than was realized. Communication and coordination among agencies were poor, particularly at central headquarters.

The complexity of the projects arose partly from the Bank's interest in adding directly productive components—small-scale food production programs in Colombia and Indonesia and food industry activities in Brazil. The decision to include them failed to take account of a principal point about the value of nutrition projects: that better nutrition makes all other sectors more productive.

In retrospect it would have been preferable to undertake less ambitious, more narrowly focused projects consisting of no more than three or four well-integrated nutrition interventions that did not require extensive managerial skills. As experience in the fourth project, in Tamil Nadu, demonstrated, freestanding nutrition projects should be limited in scope. But the Tamil Nadu project also showed that projects need not be confined to a single sector. The Colombia project demonstrated the benefit of an intersectoral effort as well—in that case the substantially increased use of primary health care facilities made possible by a nutrition intervention.

The early projects, which were planned to last four years, proved to be unrealistically short to demonstrate the expected changes in mortality and nutrition status, let alone longer-term benefits such as improved educability and productivity. Although there are exceptions (Tamil Nadu, with its advanced planning and management skills, being the best example), projects that depend on newly established institutions should have simple, straightforward goals, or they may require six to eight years to show a nutrition impact for large population groups. What may seem to be an excessively long start-up time may be necessary for success. The full year built into the Indonesian nutrition education component just to gain understanding and train local people turned out to be pivotal to a successful program. For countries that do not have experience with sizable nutrition interventions, a short preparation project may be a necessary precursor to larger, operationally oriented projects.

A blueprint cannot be written for a standard nutrition project. Mechanisms that work in a socially cohesive country such as Indonesia may not meet the needs of a society such as Tamil Nadu, where villagers may not have a tradition of doing things together. Differences in nutritional needs, causes of malnutrition, capability of human resources, and political systems dictate variations in approach, scale, type of delivery system, and ratio of servicing staff to beneficiaries. Nonetheless, certain standard methodological procedures can be applied, and some packages have been identified that are generally effective for addressing different types and causes of malnutrition under different circumstances (as described in chapter 8).

Because political interest in subjects such as nutrition can fluctuate, project planning may have to be less deliberate than a new field of activity would seem to require. In Indonesia the time-conscious government planning agency, BAPPENAS, decided to push ahead without all the answers because it believed that its program was moving in the right direction, that it could learn from experience, and that (in the words of the deputy chairman) "seizing the opportunity while there is interest and resources" would pay the greatest dividends ten years later. Such circumstances still call for starting out on a pilot scale and expanding with experience, as best exemplified by the Tamil Nadu project. Also, projects must be flexible if they are to take advantage of unanticipated opportunities that emerge during implementation.

The Institutional Framework

Since nutrition does not fit easily into any existing ministry, should a technical agency such as a ministry of health or agriculture, a supraministerial body such as a planning ministry, or a specially assigned interministerial commission be given responsibility for integrating nutrition activities into government machinery? And should nutrition projects be managed by existing agencies or by new project units?

In Colombia the National Planning Department (DNP), which had control of investment budgets, made some progress in getting line agencies to work together, thereby producing synergistic effects. For example, the health services component and the food coupon program were mutually reinforcing; distribution of the coupons by the health post personnel proved an efficient way to reach target groups, while the availability of the coupons motivated more regular attendance at the health posts. The planning staff, with its control of resources, prompted the health ministry to move toward better primary care, even though at times there was resistance from parts of the bureaucracy.

The Colombian experience pointed to the many difficulties in converting planners into implementers, in entrusting responsibility to an agency without any roots in the community, and in making a staff agency, rather than a line agency, responsible for program implementation. Focusing the efforts of diverse ministries requires an entity that is both uncommitted to parochial interests and able to provide strong direction and coordination. Experience in Brazil showed the difficulties of asking an agency within a health ministry to plan and coordinate actions of other line agencies; as in most countries, the choice of top health staff in Brazil is frequently based on medical rather than administrative reputations. Although some synergistic effects were achieved, one example being that the education and health staffs worked together on the successful PROAPE program, Brazil's coordinating agency INAN sometimes had difficulty getting from the member ministries the response contemplated by the project. Some of the same kinds of problems were seen in the Indonesia project.

Meeting with more success was the Tamil Nadu approach, which brought together effectively, through an empowered committee chaired by the state's chief secretary, the secretaries of finance, health, social welfare, and other concerned government departments. The secretary to the committee was the project coordinator, who otherwise directed a special unit established solely to administer the project day to day. A telling difference between this unit and the responsible bodies in the other projects was that the Tamil Nadu group was made up of professional administrators, a factor reflected in the efficiency of that project's implementation. To provide continuity in the ongoing program after the project would be completed, the government was careful to plan the integration of project activities into existing institutions.

During the period these projects were being implemented, several other countries established multiministerial coordinating mechanisms without a responsible ministry; generally they were not successful. The need for a strong administrative focal point to run projects is clear. The best approach appears to be a lead ministry (or under some circumstances a supraministry), its exact placement depending on the nature of the project and the practices and preferences of the government. A project that is innovative and involves several executing agencies requires, at least initially, a coordinating body located in a respected and powerful agency. In Papua New Guinea, for example, the focal point for coordinating nutrition had more influence when it was located in the ministry responsible for agriculture than when it was lodged in the ministry of health.

More important for project effectiveness than organizational form are the support and involvement of politically powerful decision-makers. (If such support and involvement do not already exist, obtaining them should be an important early objective.) The importance of governmental commitment, the fragility of it, and the difficulties of assessing it were special problems in this new area of World Bank lending. Where it existed, as in the case of Tamil Nadu, the high-level support clearly increased the willingness of participating bodies to cooperate.

Another vital ingredient is the interest and support of entities expected to participate in a project. If they are unable to build good relations, project management staff will remain outsiders, confronted with the defenses and inertia of bureaucracies not committed to cooperation. Capacity to build commitment is just as important a qualification as technical competence of staff hired for nutrition projects.

How integrated should services be? The Tamil Nadu project risked the conflicts and complications of setting up a separate system of community nutrition workers in order to avoid overburdening health care workers. The project demonstrated that, where interdepartmental cooperation is nurtured, parallel and complementary systems can work and can be mutually reinforcing. If tasks are well defined and cooperation is stressed during training and by supervisory staff, health and nutrition workers can work together effectively even when they come under the authority of different line agencies. In some circumstances, divided responsibility may be a more successful formula than overburdening community health workers with many different tasks.

Management Requirements

Good management can make the most of an unfortunate choice of organizations, and the best organizational arrangements make little difference if management is not competent. The delays in implementation and the reprogramming required in certain of the projects reflect the widespread lack of successful management experience in agencies that implement nutrition projects (and, indeed, many development projects). Unfortunately, the projects generally did not provide the time or training needed to develop managerial capability.

The complexity of the nutrition projects, except in Tamil Nadu, strained the management capabilities of implementing agencies. (Bank staff were overly optimistic in their expectations.) Had the Brazilian and Colombian groups been free to concentrate on fewer tasks, they might have done better, and more careful attention to regular communication with participating ministries might have opened opportunities for early resolution of differences that interfered with implementation and coordination of the projects.

For a variety of reasons, INAN in Brazil could hardly have been expected to succeed in its managerial role. The project's design was too ambitious, and INAN's managerial approach, which provided little communication with implementing agencies, turned out to be especially limiting. Weather, ecological, administrative, and socioeconomic factors introduced so much variability into the project that it was impossible to measure the effect of some components. But the most serious obstacle to successful management was the assignment of a weak agent of the federal government to coordinate other federal agencies and to execute a project and supervise programs that were essentially being implemented by state and local agencies.

Few attempts were made to coordinate inputs, management, or evaluation of the various project components. Even though the project unit at INAN knew what was being done in all the field components, it lacked the capacity to examine program results and build from them a national nutrition strategy as originally intended. Indeed, evaluation of the programs was eventually contracted out to the University of São Paulo's Institute for Economic Research.

In Colombia the DNP, which was responsible for managing the project, lacked the expertise to ensure that components were properly carried out. And by the admission of DNP staff itself, the department was not very effective in its role as coordinator, which involved ensuring collaboration from nearly twenty agencies in several sectors and eight jurisdictions.[a] Given the experimental nature of the project, it is especially disappointing that the DNP did not adequately evaluate the project's impact on nutrition status.[1]

The Colombian staff was overextended, with the project going into too many areas too quickly. Full coverage in a few areas was sacrificed for thin coverage nationally. Although far more investment was carried out than would have been possible if the project had expanded more slowly, more systematic expansion could have led to better services and perhaps more demonstrable effect.

In contrast, Tamil Nadu managers were able to give more effective direction. They gradually developed routine systems that helped agencies coordinate activities and permitted project workers to acquire necessary skills systematically. The Tamil Nadu project also benefited from the interest of its state and national governments in nutrition and the presence of institutions that were prepared to manage the program.

In a number of situations, the failure of the projects to ensure initially that essential administrative skills were available at all operating levels precluded effective management. Preparing budget proposals, writing contract specifications, and monitoring performance of nutrition projects through a management information system, for example, require special knowledge and skills. And World Bank requirements compounded management difficulties. In Colombia reporting disbursement of funds to the Bank was a problem throughout

a. A related point about coordination merits note here. Governments are faced with the challenge of coordinating activities undertaken with World Bank lending with those undertaken through other international agencies and nongovernmental organizations. Nationwide many nutrition projects of different agencies may be operating (in the Gambia, for example, twenty-six government and nongovernment agencies are currently active in nutrition). At a minimum, conflict among them in goals and approaches must be prevented, and ideally they should contribute to the implementation of an articulated national strategy. The lack of a central agency for nutrition complicates this problem. A mechanism for harmonizing various programs is sorely needed.

implementation and caused a two-year extension of the project. Difficulties with Bank procedures also caused delays in the Indonesia project. The workshops that are now being used to launch many Bank-supported projects address such issues and will offer a useful orientation for future nutrition projects in countries that have not previously had them.

The value of pilot activities was seen in Tamil Nadu and Indonesia, where they helped to expose implementation problems, so that the subsequent larger projects were more sensitive to political realities, bureaucratic constraints, and local needs. An underlying strength of these pilot projects, unlike many others, was that they were undertaken by agencies responsible for the subsequent larger operations and their procedures were replicable on a large scale.

Where nutrition programs have been successfully launched, strong entrepreneurial skills have invariably been evident. The ability to serve as catalyst and promote the involvement of several agencies and disciplines in a program is more important than sophisticated scientific or technical capacity in getting viable programs under way. People who can initiate and effectively manage large programs (and, preferably, who have a general grounding in nutrition) are better candidates for leadership than those of scientific prominence whose work has been largely restricted to research. The project must of course establish its professional credibility, but that can be done in many ways. Project management can be backed up by technical experts, for example, who serve on a project-specific advisory board or who hold positions elsewhere in the government and can be consulted as needed.

Monitoring and Evaluation

As in many development projects, monitoring and evaluation of the nutrition projects proved difficult. Although these components were prominent in all four of the projects, in most of the countries the value of assessing performance as a way to improve management was not widely appreciated. Neither the recording and analysis of routine data about operations nor special studies to evaluate impact were viewed as integral parts of the project's implementation. Some managers saw evaluation as a potential political threat (in one instance a dress rehearsal was held to prepare the program's beneficiaries for questions that evaluators might ask), as esoteric research, or as a minor aspect of project funding that thus deserved commensurate attention. It was seldom seen as useful to management.

Even under ideal conditions, project evaluation is technically difficult, particularly so in social sectors where behavioral factors are critical. Early experience in the nutrition projects (and similar results during the same period in rural development projects) showed that only the simplest evaluation designs should be used for large-scale projects. The evaluation study for PRAMENSE, the rural component of the Brazil nutrition project, would have been formidable to experts in a well-controlled situation. With the added complications of an unanticipated drought that led to the migration of a large part of the project sample, the evaluation exercise produced few useful results. Meanwhile, opportunities were neglected to collect routine information that would have been useful in the operations of the extension agency.

The World Bank's supervision reports, especially for the nutrition projects in Brazil and Colombia, frequently included exhortations for more attention to evaluation and suggestions for additional data collection and analysis. Less ambitious aspirations might have produced better outcomes.

In their efforts to gather sophisticated data called for in the impact studies, central monitoring units failed to build the capacity in field units to collect simple operating data routinely and accurately or the capacity in managerial offices to interpret and respond to the data. Once operations staff perceived the evaluators' biases toward longer-term policy-oriented studies over those more immediately useful for program needs, the evaluators' effectiveness was diminished. Analysis of the Colombia experience by a DNP staff member concluded that one of the shortcomings of that project was the lack of quick studies that could have led to rapid midcourse operational corrections. The need was seen, in retrospect, to "define a small number of impact indicators clearly and insure the necessary time period, sample size, financial resources and manpower to obtain them." To gain broad acceptance for the project, this analysis goes on to suggest the need to make use of the outcomes of the studies with press, politicians, and professional groups.[2]

Much of the monitoring and evaluation work in the nutrition projects fell behind schedule or below acceptable standards. There are examples, however, of work of good quality: Indonesia's evaluation of the nutrition education component and its revised system for monitoring NIPP, monitoring and evaluation in Tamil Nadu, Colombia's evaluation of the primary health care program, and Brazil's evaluation of PINS, which resulted in the program's modification. Efforts to institutionalize the art and practice of evaluation generally got under way much more slowly than had been expected and in some cases fared poorly.

Helping countries expand their evaluation horizons and skills requires more time than the nutrition projects permitted. Sensitivity to the need for monitoring and evaluation did increase, however, and substantial progress was reported. And the mistakes and problems of each early project served as guides in planning for monitoring and evaluation of subsequent projects, hence the complex, research-oriented design of the Brazil evaluation component and the simpler, more effective design of the Tamil Nadu component.

Inadequate commitment to and understanding of the evaluation process among local managers, scarcity of analytical skills, technical difficulties, neglect of monitoring, and poor understanding of the relationship of monitoring to evaluation are common problems—observers of rural development projects in East Asia, for instance, reported that "information has seldom been used effectively."[3] In other sectors in which the World Bank supports projects, the ultimate effect on the well-being of project beneficiaries is seldom evaluated;[4] process indicators are commonly used as proxies for impact. In attempting to assess the changes in physical growth resulting from their programs, the nutrition projects exceeded the evaluation goals of other sectors by a considerable margin.

Future nutrition projects should follow the example of Tamil Nadu in keeping reasonable expectations about monitoring and evaluation. Data from a number of nutrition centers in Tamil Nadu were surveyed each quarter to keep the amount of information manageable and to determine what was necessary for reliable monitoring.

Evaluation should be encouraged as a way to improve programs, not as a judgment of the performance of project personnel. A sound and workable monitoring and evaluation system should be adopted at the outset of a project, with due regard for the need to use some segment of the population for comparison purposes. (This is a delicate ethical issue, but the work in these projects has demonstrated that studies can be set up that do not work to the disadvantage of the group being used for comparison.) Data should be collected routinely from the beginning and should be limited to what is most needed. Intermediate outcomes should not be neglected since they help operating staff make needed adjustments as the project progresses. Intermediate outcomes also help develop an appreciation of the value of sound monitoring and evaluation. Finally, an evaluation should recognize that the project is not likely to be attempting to alleviate all the various constraints to improved nutrition, even though the design of the project needs to take those other determinants of malnutrition into account.

Future nutrition projects should concentrate initially on determining whether systems can deliver on an operational scale the services that have had positive effects in well-controlled, small-scale studies. Later efforts should try to evaluate the impact of projects on the nutrition status of the targeted population. This pattern is also espoused now for health projects.

5 | Nutrition Actions in Other Projects

BESIDES SUPPORTING nutrition projects, the World Bank can address nutrition issues through two other channels in its project work. One is to design and fund nutrition components in projects in other sectors. The second is to build nutrition considerations into the orientation of other projects. By including such considerations from the planning stage, projects (in agriculture, for instance) can improve nutrition status along with their other goals or, at least, minimize the possibility of harming nutrition inadvertently. The potential of either channel has not been realized.

Nutrition Components

In the late 1970s the Bank concentrated on incorporating nutrition components and subcomponents into projects in other sectors. These required considerably less staff time to prepare and supervise than whole projects devoted to nutrition, yet they appeared to offer a means of introducing nutrition ideas to national leaders and achieving the broader objectives of nutrition projects. This approach is exemplified in a component of a project in Thailand.

Nutrition in a Population Project

Despite generally good food supplies, Thailand for years has had a serious problem of malnutrition among infants and preschool children in poor families. A nationwide surveillance program found that 50 percent of preschool children were malnourished by Thai standards. The government had on several occasions tried to combat the problem through supplementary feeding programs tied to health services. They reached only a fraction of those at risk, however.

70

In 1979 a different approach was adopted as a part of a Bank-assisted population project. In some ninety villages in three northeastern provinces where malnutrition was most marked, villagers were encouraged to form cooperatives to run their own programs. Village health volunteers and communicators were responsible for conducting monthly weighings of all infants and preschool children. Mothers were responsible for monitoring the weights and keeping their children's weight charts, and workers helped them learn when the children needed supplementary feeding. Once or twice a week each mother took her children and some rice to a village lunch at which a food supplement, locally grown and prepared for the program, was served.

The cooperatives also produced nutrition supplements—simple mixtures of rice and mung beans, rice and soybeans, or groundnuts and sesame seeds—that were packaged and provided free for children with moderate or severe malnutrition. Any excess production could be sold to families with healthier children and to neighboring villages, and the proceeds were put back into the program or other community development activities. About half of the cooperatives became self-supporting.

The results of the nutrition action program were dramatic, according to the director general of the Thai Department of Health. Mild malnutrition declined rapidly, and moderate and severe malnutrition virtually disappeared in participating villages. The program worked for two reasons. First, mothers gained a fuller understanding that their children's health depended on a proper diet (for themselves during pregnancy and lactation and for their infants and young children). Second, the whole community—mothers, farmers, health workers, teachers, and others—got involved in helping to reduce malnutrition.[1]

The rural program was so successful that it was expanded in 1982 to cover 2,000 villages as part of the national development program for impoverished areas. By 1986, 60 percent of all Thai villages had a nutrition program, with participation rates commonly between 80 and 90 percent of eligible preschool children.

Other Population and Health Projects

Growth monitoring and nutrition education have been the main nutrition activities of population and health projects. Health projects have seldom included full nutrition components because the projects have usually been concerned with developing infrastructure or improving management. But primary health care or maternal and child health programs within larger projects have frequently included nutrition actions.

Assessment of nutrition status was part of a community health care component of a Peruvian health project. Nutrition education was part of the component to strengthen basic health services in a health project in Senegal and part of broader communications components in projects in Indonesia, the Philippines, and Tunisia. Often in such programs the distinction between nutrition and health components becomes blurred, so that what started as a nutrition intervention becomes a standard part of the health care repertoire—both growth monitoring and oral rehydration therapy, for example, are actions devised by the nutrition community.

Some projects have had more discrete nutrition components. A large and apparently effective mass media promotion of breastfeeding was conducted under a Jamaican population and nutrition project. (Data from national surveys independent of the project found that the mean duration of breastfeeding increased from ten to thirteen months during the project. Because the planned evaluation of this program was never completed, a causal link with the project cannot be confirmed.[2]) And an Indian population project included a nutrition education effort that had positive effects on nutrition awareness and dietary practices; distribution of food supplements under the same project had a minimal effect on nutrition, however. A component of a health project in the Yemen Arab Republic established a nutrition unit in the Ministry of Health to plan and coordinate food and nutrition activities.

Urban Development Projects

Bank-assisted urban development projects have incorporated training of paramedical workers in nutrition, surveys or surveillance of nutrition status, and actions addressing specific nutrient deficiencies. Projects for upgrading urban slums have usually provided for building, equipping, and expanding health posts, clinics, and centers that can diagnose and treat malnutrition and provide nutrition education in conjunction with standard health services. Community centers built through the projects also can be used for nutrition education and child development activities. And some of these projects have provided for construction of markets that can improve access to food or help lower food prices.

A Tanzanian project included a $1.1 million nutrition component that provided two nutrition and garden centers and ten demonstration gardens. Extension services, nutrition education, and cooking classes were established in the centers to encourage poultry-keeping and cultivation of fruit trees and vegetables; seedlings, insecticides, and tools were sold there as well. That program was popular enough for the centers to become self-supporting.

A health and nutrition program included in a Calcutta urban development project identified malnourished participants and provided supplementary feeding and nutrition education in nutrition clinics. The Indian government later extended the program to 2 million *bustee* (shanty) and slum dwellers, a tenfold increase in coverage. A similar effort, on a smaller scale, was undertaken in a Bank-assisted project in Madras. In Bolivia a component of an urban development project enlisted high school students to follow up clinic patients to ensure the return of those who needed further nutrition or health care. The students' commitment to the task and the low administrative costs apparently led to the request to expand the component.

Agriculture and Rural Development Projects

Agriculture and rural development projects have promoted home gardens, small fish ponds, food fortification, food technology centers, growth monitoring and treatment of nutritionally vulnerable groups, nutrition education, and surveys and training for future programs. In Papua New Guinea an agricultural support services project provided staff for the Food and Nutrition Planning unit in the Department of Primary Industry (Agriculture), which serves as the focal point for nutrition in that country.

Nutrition status surveys that were components of a fisheries project in the People's Democratic Republic of Yemen and a grain storage and processing project in the Yemen Arab Republic were successful enough to inspire follow-on activities. A nutrition extension program included in a rural development project in Peru was sufficiently well executed that it was offered to 50 percent more villages than planned. A Philippines rainfed agricultural development project included anemia control and diarrhea management programs as well as nutrition monitoring and evaluation, and an agricultural support services project in the Philippines financed the establishment of a food and nutrition unit in the Ministry of Agriculture to assess nutrition needs and to design policies and programs for a national food and nutrition plan. That project also undertook a national food and nutrition survey and pilot nutrition programs for municipalities. An agricultural development project in Ghana offered home extension work, including promotion of home gardens and reduction of food waste, to five districts. And in Brazil all of the rural development projects in the Northeast included social extension, part of which is nutrition education.

A rural development project in Mauritius that developed kitchen gardens (described in chapter 2) also included rabbit rearing, which was somewhat less successful than the gardens (the rabbits' mortality rate was 47 percent). Nonetheless, more than a third of the families claimed that their nutrition had improved and that their income had increased 10 percent from rabbit sales.

A rural services project in Rwanda included a nutrition component for monitoring malnutrition, determining its causes, and assessing the impact of remedial measures. That component became a field laboratory for exploring alternative approaches to nutrition improvement. Its results were used in preparing a recently approved project in family health that contains a substantial nutrition component.

Education Projects

Nutrition education has been included as a part of education projects in the Syrian Arab Republic and Togo, and in the former country the program has focused on the quality of school feeding. In Morocco, 15,000 school canteens were constructed through an education loan. And education projects in Northeast Brazil have financed the construction and equipping of warehouses and the purchase of vehicles to improve the efficiency of the school feeding program.

Complementing Components

Some nutrition components of projects in other sectors have been designed to complement the actions of a nutrition project. The first nutrition project in Indonesia and its follow-on nutrition and community health project benefited from several parallel projects: a health manpower project built facilities to provide nutrition training for government staff; an education project included postgraduate studies in nutrition and related research; a transmigration project included funding for home gardens for all new settlers; and population and health projects included sizable funding for nutrition actions in villages.

The Lessons

The Bank's experience with nutrition components has been uneven. Some helpful work has been undertaken. But, unfortunately, many opportunities have already been missed, and some attempts have been too limited in scope. Rarely has the cost of nutrition components exceeded 5 percent of the total in projects in other sectors. Because of their size, nutrition components have received little attention from national governments, particularly if problems in the administration of larger components impede implementation of the project. For the same reason nutrition components have often been neglected by World Bank staff.

Monitoring and evaluating nutrition components may have suffered because they seemed too small to merit much effort. Bank staff overseeing the parent projects have sometimes lacked the technical familiarity, time, or interest. As a result, they could provide only limited assistance to those trying to implement the components.

In urban projects efforts to encourage community participation in neighborhood improvements, including nutrition efforts, have strengthened community cohesion and have helped to recover costs, ensure maintenance, and improve social services. In some cases community support has been effective, though time-consuming; in others neighborhood politics have been beyond the reach of the Bank and collaborating institutions.[3] The experience of urban projects, like that of nutrition projects, generally points to the advantages of simplification. As a result, the number of special health and nutrition components in urban projects has decreased.

Though the preparation and supervision of nutrition components has proved to be relatively inexpensive, these components have seldom addressed the most important nutrition problems in a country or operated in the areas of greatest nutrition need; their nature and location are necessarily dictated by their parent project. In many instances they have done little to promote discussion of nutrition policies or to build institutions. Nonetheless, the success of some components shows that they can be designed and carried out in ways that can contribute to nutrition improvement.

Nutrition Considerations

Building nutrition considerations into the design of appropriate agriculture and rural development projects is potentially more important than adding nutrition components to these projects. A 1980 review of nutrition by the World Bank's Policy Review Committee concluded that (a) when economic and sector analyses conclude that agriculture-related interventions can make a central contribution to meeting chronic nutrition needs, projects should be considered toward that end, and (b) in projects aimed at improving the well-being of low-income groups, nutrition should be added as an explicit objective, where feasible. Project planners should include nutrition considerations in their judgments of what crops to emphasize in research, storage, and extension projects.

A Bank agricultural research policy paper a year later called for "Bank-assisted agricultural research projects [to] give increased attention to nutritional implications of food production systems and, where appropriate, emphasize research on foods of major importance in the diets of the poor."[4]

Determining whether significant nutrition effects can be obtained without causing unacceptable changes in other areas is a policy question, but tradeoffs among conflicting goals need to be considered explicitly. At a minimum, projects were to be examined to ensure that their effect on food supply, food prices, or incomes did not worsen the nutrition status of the project's beneficiaries or other groups. Projects judged to have potentially deleterious effects were either to be reoriented or to have nutrition components added to offset the negative effects.

Guidelines were developed for incorporating nutrition considerations in the Bank's agriculture sector work.[5] Several Bank studies extensively analyzed food consumption issues (in, for example, China, Haiti, Morocco, and Nigeria), and several agriculture projects were designed with major attention directed to meet nutrition needs. The main objective of rural development projects in Nepal and Papua New Guinea was to increase food consumption levels of the poor to meet standard nutrition requirements; all of the main components flowed from this objective. Another project in Papua New Guinea, which encouraged a shift from subsistence farming to cash crops (primarily coffee and tea), provided extension services to increase production in family food gardens and other assurances to offset the project's potentially negative effects on nutrition. And a resettlement project in Malaysia, as part of a long-term program for planting rubber trees, set aside land for food crops, built and stocked community fish ponds, and offered nutrition education.

Generally, however, nutrition has not been well integrated into the framework of Bank-assisted agriculture and rural development projects. Agriculture specialists working on these projects, both from the countries and from the Bank, have often assumed that the way to address malnutrition is to increase food supply, and they have regarded more complex nutrition issues as social welfare problems outside their domain. Or these staff have not had time to deal with nutrition issues (or, in some cases, the training to feel comfortable doing so). Though malnutrition is sometimes used to justify agriculture projects, nutrition goals are rarely included explicitly. And governments often lack the interest or capability to work for their inclusion.

Health sector analyses commonly identify malnutrition as a principal reason for poor health. It seems logical to include nutrition in the planning and implementation of health programs, not only because inadequate nutrition is so much a part of the health problem, but because the interaction of malnutrition and infection has more serious results than the effects of either independently.[a] Yet sizable actions to counter nutrition problems have not, until recently, been regularly incorporated in health projects. This omission reflects judgments that many projects (especially those that emphasize infrastructure) would not seem to accommodate nutrition components easily,[b] that solving malnutrition problems would fall outside the ministry of health's jurisdiction, or that adding a nutrition dimension would add unmanageable complexity to a project. It also reflects the priority of popu-

a. For example, diarrheal disease is strongly associated with decreased absorption of energy, protein, and micronutrients. In addition, a sick child has a diminished appetite in spite of increased needs, and caretakers may withhold food as a form of treatment, which jeopardizes the child's health and nutrition status even more.
b. In fact, early considerations of the need for nutrition services might influence the nature and design of health facilities and equipment—just as it should influence training programs, logistic systems, and health information systems.

lation projects in the work program of project officers in the World Bank's Department of Population, Health, and Nutrition and, in some instances, the lack of familiarity with the techniques and tools to incorporate nutrition.[6]

There is now increased understanding that health projects are not going to work—that mortality and morbidity objectives will not be achieved—without addressing malnutrition, where it is an important contributor to poor health. Nutrition, therefore, needs to be more than just another action to be considered for inclusion in primary health care; in many instances it may be a prerequisite for the fulfillment of broader health objectives. Similarly, objectives of population projects to reduce fertility are unlikely to be met so long as mortality rates run high and families continue to perceive the need for many children.[7]

ALTHOUGH there are exceptions, by and large the efforts to add a nutrition dimension to activities of the World Bank in other sectors have not been as successful as they might have been. This result probably flows from inadequacies in design (including inappropriate coverage), promotion, and follow-through in the Bank; limitations of staff time and interest; and concern by staff that the complexity of projects be decreased. It also reflects, however, the way the Bank is structured and staffed along sectoral lines—nutrition cuts across sectors—and the nature of the Bank's system for assessing and rewarding staff. That the same patterns of compartmentalization are observed in many borrowing countries compounds the problem, making it easy for nutrition to slip through organizational cracks.

6 | Analytic Work in Nutrition

EARLY NUTRITION EFFORTS in many countries had been hampered by a lack of understanding of the causes of malnutrition and the policies and projects needed to deal with it. Thus at the same time that the World Bank undertook a few priority large-scale actions and evaluations of those actions, it also undertook studies on the impact of policies, programs, and projects on nutrition and the effect of improvements in nutrition on human capital and economic growth. At the country level, the emphasis was on nutrition sector work that might be useful in understanding country-specific problems and, where appropriate, in laying the groundwork for nutrition operations.

Analysis of Specific Countries

The Bank's Policy Review Committee decided in 1980 to give more emphasis to nutrition in country economic and sector work, so that Bank staff could better incorporate nutrition into operational work and policy dialogues with member countries. Guidelines were drawn up for nutrition sector analyses, and by late 1983 twenty-one reviews dealing with the nutrition problems of sixteen countries had been completed. The reviews varied in depth; a few scanned the subject only lightly.

Comparing the Country Studies

Despite the differences in the countries examined, their nutrition problems, and the scope, intensity, and quality of the sector analyses, studies of nine of the countries provided strong evidence of serious problems—moderate or severe malnutrition among a significant fraction of children and undernourishment among a nontrivial fraction of adults, compounded by micronutrient deficiencies. The principal problem was lack of sufficient energy in the diet. For some countries (such as the Philippines and Zimbabwe) the problem was not only the amount of food intake but also the density of the calories consumed.[a] Seasonal malnutrition was found to be particularly important in Burkina Faso, Indonesia, Lesotho, Rwanda, Senegal, Zambia, and Zimbabwe. Whether the problem was one of supply or demand—stemming from swings in food production or from seasonal changes in income—was not clear.

In a few countries in which food consumption was rising, portions of the population (estimated at 15 percent in Indonesia, certainly higher in others) were found to be lagging badly. The nutrition status of the poorest groups in Peru and the Yemen Arab Republic was found to have deteriorated over time. In Indonesia and Nigeria changes in the price of food were thought to have caused a deterioration in nutrition status (income movements were also suggested).

An increase in income, either in cash or in kind, was in some cases found to be a necessary condition for improvement in the nutrition status of adults and an important condition for improvement in children. In countries in which the largest nutritionally distressed groups were rural people with access to land, the greatest potential for public policy appeared to be in increasing the productivity of that land, stimulating rural employment, ensuring appropriate farmgate food prices, and targeting attention to malnourished children.

In several cases the sector analyses suggested that malnutrition was not confined to the lowest income group. In Brazil, for instance, increases in income and in food purchases did not correspond closely (malnutrition was observed among families who used discretionary income to buy television sets and other durable goods), and in the Yemen Arab Republic deleterious child-feeding practices and poor dietary selection and preparation habits persisted even though incomes went up.

A common problem was the tension between a pricing policy that

a. Foods with very low energy density (that is, low concentrations of calories or energy per unit of weight), such as cassava and plantains, may require consumption of exorbitant amounts just to meet energy requirements, particularly in the case of young children. See Food and Agriculture Organization, *Dietary Fats and Oils in Human Nutrition*, FAO Food and Nutrition Paper 3 (Rome, 1977), p. 8.

encouraged domestic food production and a nutrition policy that aimed at keeping retail prices of food grains at a level the poor could afford. Pakistan, with a two-track subsidy system that benefited both producers and consumers, seemed to come closest to dealing effectively with this dilemma.

One of the surprises that emerged from the sector work was how quickly people could shift their preferences from traditional, locally produced grains (for example, millet and sorghum in Nigeria and Yemen) to polished rice and refined wheat, both often imported. Administered prices favoring the new products underlay the shift in many cases. This policy raised the possibilities of reduced food security, a decline in expenditure on domestically produced grains (and thus in rural income), and vitamin and mineral problems stemming from a shift to highly processed grain (as in Zambia and Zimbabwe). This potentially serious nutrition danger argues forcefully for the need to consider the implications for nutrition of price policy measures. Well-chosen price policies can have a positive effect on nutrition status.

No clear conclusions emerged from the sector work about efforts to manipulate agricultural prices explicitly to achieve nutrition objectives. Household studies showed that food purchases varied in response to changes in prices. Where possibly negative effects of agricultural production strategies on malnourished groups were considered, the sectoral reports did not clearly demonstrate a relation between specific policies and decreased consumption.

Despite the recognized power of the mass media to affect tastes and behavior, it is noteworthy that with few exceptions (such as Zambia) country studies made no mention of efforts to use mass media to change deleterious diet and child-feeding practices that appear to be independent of household budget constraints. A study of the nutritional adequacy of family diets in Indonesia found that relatively affluent households with relatively educated homemakers opted for expensive foods even at some sacrifice in needed nutrients. In Zimbabwe the sector work pointed up the importance of directing nutrition education efforts not only at women, but also at men, given their control over family resources.

In countries with reasonably effective delivery systems, sector reviews identified a variety of successful direct nutrition interventions: Brazil's requirement that companies make provision for women employees to breastfeed their infants; Zimbabwe's supplementary feeding programs for children; Rwanda's network of nutrition centers for surveillance, rehabilitation, supplementation, and related activities; Pakistan's consumer food subsidies; China's support of a minimum consumption level; and Zambia's mass media effort to change child-feeding practices. They also identified unsuccessful interventions, such as protein enrichment in India (when the greater problem was low energy intake) and consumer subsidies on the wrong foods in Zimbabwe.

The sector analyses convey a strong sense of nutritionists' reliance on other disciplines and organizations to carry out nutrition efforts. A relatively narrow track appears to exist for delivering nutrition services independently. Thus it is important to infuse nutrition considerations into areas that affect nutrition and to develop food and nutrition focal points and coordinating processes in government.

Twelve of the reviews of national nutrition problems provided useful information for formulating World Bank–supported projects, six were fair guides, and three were poor. Some of the studies provided new insights for governments or into particular situations. The work on eight of the countries contributed at least to some modest extent to the development of government policies or the formulation of projects to be supported by the Bank or another donor, and a brief survey of one country led to a decision not to explore the sector further.[1]

Sector work on Brazil appears to have been useful in national planning; the government cited it in policy documents and later requested an update of the findings. In Indonesia the Bank's sector work was used in planning the food and nutrition component of the country's five-year plan. Sector work on the Yemen Arab Republic contributed to that government's decision to establish a nutrition planning unit; work on Zimbabwe was a factor in changing the emphasis on particular crops in a Bank-aided agriculture project; work on Nigeria encouraged the government to carry out a national nutrition survey in preparation for discussions with the Bank on a possible nutrition operation; and work on Burkina Faso helped to shape plans for a similar survey there.

The World Bank's sector work contributed to the design of the Philippine Food and Nutrition Plan (which was the main topic at a meeting of a donor consortium for that country), provided a basis for the establishment of a nutrition planning unit in the Ministry of Agriculture, and prompted a national survey of food consumption and nutrition (aided by Bank project lending in agriculture). The minister of agriculture gave the plan credit for leading to pilot work in consumer food subsidies. In China the sector work broadened consideration of the nutritional value of different foods in agricultural work and prompted inclusion of malnutrition as a health problem in discussions with the Chinese.

Building a Nutrition Information Base

In many countries data on nutrition are so limited that the standard sector analysis is unlikely to expose many issues of consequence. As a shortcut to understanding nutrition conditions and what causes those conditions, unorthodox approaches have been found to be useful. In Zimbabwe in 1982, for instance, a World Bank staff member, in addition to searching the literature, spent a month in the field collecting "best judgments" from a variety of knowledgeable observers.[2]

Brief questionnaires sent to government health field staff and doctors of religious missions and other nongovernmental operations asked simple questions such as how prevalent they sensed specific nutrition deficiencies to be in their areas ("often," "sometimes," "seldom," or "never"?). Similarly, agricultural extension field staff were asked for their judgments about the sufficiency of food in their areas, the variation in seasonal needs, and the causes of poor nutrition. In addition, medical school students were mobilized to make spot nutrition surveys in different parts of the country, and "snapshot" surveys of food consumption and nutrition status were added to studies already planned on agricultural production and income.

Regression analysis was used to relate information on nutrition status to data on production, income, and expenditures, which had been collected for other purposes. Also the detailed data collected on two areas in the late 1970s were analyzed and compared with information available at the time of independence.

It was quickly evident that, despite being a substantial food exporter, Zimbabwe had a major malnutrition problem. More than 20 percent of children less than five years old suffered from second- or third-degree malnutrition and nearly 30 percent were stunted (a characteristic that implies chronic undernutrition). Kwashiorkor and marasmus, which are the most severe forms of energy-protein malnutrition and so uncommon in most nonfamine conditions as to be medical curiosities, were frequently seen in Zimbabwean health facilities.

The most serious nutrition problems were found among children in families of commercial farm workers, followed by those in communally farmed areas. There were significant seasonal differences, with the worst period being October through December, when food is in shortest supply. The greatest prevalence of malnutrition was in children seven to twenty-four months old. The problem appeared to be primarily a shortage of calories rather than of protein, with caloric density an added problem for small children. Vitamin and mineral deficiency disorders, particularly pellagra and goiter, were much more prevalent than had been generally believed. (From the best judgments of the 149 observers it was possible, for instance, to begin mapping the incidence of goiter.)

A large portion of the population produced too little food to meet its needs, and incomes of commercial farm workers and most families in communal areas were clearly inadequate to satisfy nutrition requirements. Moreover, the shifts in diet that accompanied modernization were not always nutritionally advantageous.

The understanding of nutrition concepts and needs among rural women was better than they were given credit for. The principal gap was in knowing the number of feedings a day required by a small child on a diet primarily of *sadza*, a local porridge based on corn. Infection seems not to play as large a role in malnutrition in Zimbabwe as in most countries (which may account for the relatively low infant and child mortality rates in Zimbabwe). Alcoholism, family separations, and other social problems do play a role, particularly in cases of kwashiorkor and marasmus.

A considerable number of nutrition-related actions were under way by both government and nongovernment agencies. Their potential was limited, however, by the lack of an official policy and central coordination. Perhaps a dozen activities in nutrition education promoted different and sometimes conflicting messages.

The program with the greatest potential for affecting nutrition—consumer food subsidies—instead of contributing to greater equity may unintentionally have had quite the opposite effect by inappropriately favoring some foods consumed heavily by other than low-income groups. Most important, there was no effective focal point in government for formulating and pressing support for proposals that link production measures with consumption issues. World Bank experience indicates that solving this problem is essential for an effective policy dealing with malnutrition. The single most important need was for a nutrition policy and strategy. In the absence of an official statement of objectives and how to achieve them, malnutrition meant different things to different people. This, in turn, led to a variety of intervention programs with different and sometimes conflicting objectives.

Yet, Zimbabwe is better equipped than most African countries to address malnutrition. Among its assets are relatively sophisticated services, capable staff, good support from voluntary agencies and universities, good community organization, and, most important, government interest and commitment to deal with the problem. These assets and a general outline of the country's nutrition problems allowed the principal nutrition needs to be assessed and suggested the interventions necessary to meet those needs.

Research on Nutrition in Development

Pioneering attempts by World Bank staff to disaggregate food intake of various income groups have led to the conclusion that nutrition problems are unlikely to be solved in the usual course of development, even with a substantial expansion of food production. A study on the prevalence of deficient diets concluded that in all forty countries reviewed, over half the population consumes less than the average number of calories that an expert committee of the United Nations World Health Organization (WHO) and the Food and Agriculture Organization (FAO) regards as needed to maintain moderate activity and normal functioning.[3] Another study found, as expected, that the incidence of low intake was higher among children than among the rest of the population; in Latin America the proportion of disadvantaged children was found to be double that of adults.[4] Other research, based on levels of nutrition required for survival (rather than desirable daily functioning), has estimated that those at nutritional risk are fewer but poorer than is generally believed.[5]

Notwithstanding the differences in estimations of magnitude, the studies converge in suggesting that many nutrition problems will not be solved without special measures, such as food programs and intervention in food markets, to reduce the severity of malnutrition and reach certain segments of the malnourished. One study estimated that with no change in income distribution or real food prices, per capita income growth rates in Bangladesh and Indonesia would have to exceed 5 percent annually to close the nutrition gap by bringing 95 percent of the population up to calorie requirements by the year 1995. This contrasted with historical growth rates of −0.4 percent for Bangladesh and 3.4 percent for Indonesia.[6] Another study of Bangladesh, Brazil, India, Indonesia, Morocco, and Pakistan concluded that only in Pakistan could it be expected that the entire population could enjoy adequate diets within less than thirty years. In the other countries, underfeeding of some segment of the population would persist for generations, even under optimistic prospects.[7] These and other Bank studies point out that although in some instances expanded food production is essential to eliminate malnutrition, it is not necessarily sufficient.

Linking Nutrition and Health

One of the most devastating effects of malnutrition is the way it heightens susceptibility to infectious diseases, which in turn increase the body's need for energy and decrease its ability to absorb food and recover from infection. Research on parasitic infections, undertaken in a World Bank study of iron deficiency anemia in Kenya, found that heavy ascaris infections caused the loss of as much as 20 percent of the calories victims ingested. Such a loss contributed to malnutrition and reduced the effectiveness of food supplementation programs.[8]

Analysis of data from the health and nutrition study in Narangwal, India, showed a strong relation between food intake and body size and concluded that nutrition care can reduce mortality among infants and children less than two years of age. The study measured the average costs of providing nutrition services to a young child in sufficient quantities to avert death (a range of $7.75–101.45, depending on the type of intervention and the age of the child), to avert a day of illness ($0.35–0.56), to gain an extra centimeter in growth ($26.25–30.40), and to increase psychomotor scores by a percentage point ($5.05–13.60).[9]

An examination for the Bank of ten field projects that combined nutrition and health services concluded that such programs in the hands of able administrators and in populations as large as 60,000–70,000 can reduce infant and child mortality by a third to a half in one to five years.[10] The cost would be less than 2 percent of per capita income, which is no greater than the current cost of health care.

Linking Nutrition and Economic Performance

Research by the World Bank in recent years has helped to estimate the social benefits and economic value of improved nutrition. Such work cannot begin to convey the human costs of malnutrition. Emphasis, however, was given to the socioeconomic aspects of the problem, both because work in this area has been neglected and because few of the technical agencies working in nutrition had broad experience with economic analysis.

Although nutrition status is by no means the only factor affecting productivity, it is a critical one and may be necessary for other incentives to operate effectively. The Bank's analysis of the costs and benefits of treating iron deficiency anemia in Indonesia indicated that the productivity of workers in a study group that was given iron supplements for two months increased 15 to 25 percent. The potential increase in productivity for a full-scale program was estimated to be worth as much as $260 for each dollar invested in iron supplementation.[11] In Kenya provision of extra iron and treatment of hookworm proved to be an inexpensive and feasible means of raising hemoglobin levels, so that the body could take in more of the oxygen necessary for muscular activity. Analysis indicated that the benefits of deworming undertaken twice a year could be as high as ten times the cost. Food supplementation increased road workers' productivity by 13 percent.[12] Similar studies in India found no relationship between road workers' current food intake and work output, but found a positive relationship between output and good nutrition status, as reflected in weight for height and arm circumference.[13] There are indications from other Bank studies that benefits from the reduction of iron deficiency anemia exceed costs in some cases by wide margins.[14]

Studies of how malnutrition in infants and children affects their future earning capacity and contribution to economic growth have focused on school attendance and performance.[b] Nepalese children whose height was less than 70 percent of the norm were found, after

b. Severe malnutrition can be related to mental impairment; mild and moderate malnutrition are associated with alteration in cognitive processes. Examples are passivity, apathy, shortened attention span, reduced short-term memory, failure to acclimate to repetitive stimuli, and a lag in the development of sensory-integrative capacity. These dysfunctions prevent children from taking maximum advantage of their learning environments. See Beryl Levinger, *School Feeding Programs in Developing Countries: An Analysis of Actual and Potential Impact*, Agency for International Development Evaluation Special Study 30 (Washington, D.C., 1986), p. viii.

accounting for income differences, to be 14 times less likely to be enrolled in school than children whose height was 85 percent of the norm and 228 times less likely than those whose height equaled the norm.[15] A similar relationship was found for weight: children at 70 percent of the norm were four times less likely to be enrolled in school than those at 85 percent of the norm and thirteen times less likely than those at the norm. The relationship between height and weight and school enrollment was much stronger for boys than girls. These findings are consistent with those for three provinces in China where data collected by Bank staff showed that low height for age was consistently related inversely to performance, as measured by the number of grades a child was behind his age group.[16] Studies in Brazil showed a 15 percent advantage in school performance among those who were part of a preschool nutrition program,[17] and a study in Colombia showed significant effects on children's diet, growth, and school performance as a result of both nutrition supplementation and home education for mothers.[18]

Another study concluded that "supplementary feeding, if it results in a relatively modest 10 percent increase in productivity, is economically justifiable."[19] The study found that benefits are likely to be greatest when the target children get rations near their complete nutrition requirements and the children are fed on site for only two or three months. That approach was later adopted by the Tamil Nadu nutrition project, whose economic and social benefits were estimated to range between 10 and 22 percent.

Deriving Policy Guidance

Subsidized food prices and distribution policies in Bangladesh, India, Indonesia, Pakistan, and Sri Lanka were found to have eliminated between 16 and 59 percent of the gap between the number of calories consumed and that considered adequate for everyone in those countries.[20] The economic cost of programs was divided between the agricultural sector and the government, with concessional food aid greatly reducing fiscal costs in some countries. The share borne by the agricultural sector varied, with Indian farmers carrying a large share of costs and farmers in Sri Lanka a relatively small share.

A study of a ration shop scheme in India concluded that "in spite of the fact that it tends to distort prices from the competitive market values, the complex tradeoffs in the present system ultimately result in positive net social benefits for the country, if it is assumed that there is reasonable social concern for minimum food consumption of the poor."[21] The authors advocated expansion of the system if more stringent and effective eligibility requirements could be imposed and recommended that ration shops be set up in rural as well as urban areas.

Sri Lanka's rice ration program, according to one study, was directly and dramatically linked to food and nutritional adequacy and low death rate.[22] A later examination of Sri Lanka's food stamp program concluded that, if the stamp value remained constant as food prices rose, food consumption would decline, and nutrition status would deteriorate.[c] Stamp values, the author proposed, should be fully indexed to price increases, and the first group to benefit should be households in the lowest 20 percent of the income distribution.[23] An analysis of food policy in Bangladesh, India, and Zambia concluded that public interventions "are frequently of benefit only to urban groups (but often including the poorest among them)." The study also argued that "there is scope for manipulating the supply and prices of basic food staples to produce cheap calories for the poor."[24]

A review of the effects of agricultural policies and projects on nutrition concluded that "some, perhaps many, agricultural projects have had adverse nutritional outcomes." Without quantification, however, it is difficult to show whether those effects canceled the agricultural benefits.[25] Research now under way on the effects of a dairy development scheme on food consumption and nutrition in two Indian states may help to answer the question.[26]

A survey of efforts to incorporate nutrition concerns in the preparation of agricultural projects concluded that, although a number of agencies have shown interest, "very little has yet been accomplished."[27]

Measuring Cost-Effectiveness and Demand

A pioneering World Bank study, *Malnutrition and Poverty*, by Shlomo Reutlinger and Marcelo Selowsky, estimated the cost of

---

c. This prediction was later borne out when inflation reduced the real value of the food stamps, as well as wages. The effect was a decline in real incomes and calorie consumption for lower-expenditure groups. Levels of malnutrition, as measured by acute wasting, were higher after the policy change. See David E. Sahn, *Malnutrition and Food Consumption in Sri Lanka: An Analysis of Changes from 1969 to 1982* (Washington, D.C.: International Food Policy Research Institute, 1986).

achieving a given consumption increase in various food subsidy programs. It concluded that certain "target group–oriented food programs in urban areas and programs to assist low-income farm families to increase and stabilize production of food for their own consumption can be more cost-effective than outright income distribution."[28] A study of a Chilean project found that young children got more calories and protein through a supplementary food program than would be expected in an income transfer program of the same size.[29] Another study concluded that in many programs the effects were no larger than an equivalent income transfer.[30] Cash transfer programs, however, may not be the better choice because they are politically difficult to introduce and maintain. They are also likely to miss much of the target group or to benefit other groups disproportionately. The efficiency of income in the form of a food transfer is influenced by whether the food provided is purchased by the government or is part of a food aid program from abroad. Donated food may constitute an important income transfer, and generally this particular help is not available in the form of cash aid.

A study of the cost of eliminating energy gaps in Colombia, India, and Senegal over a period of twenty years indicated that specific subsidies would be less costly than general subsidies. Subsidies on local staples traditionally consumed by the poor would be least costly and most likely to benefit the target group.[31]

A 1979 study introduced the idea of a social demand function to take account of any difference between the market value and the social value of a particular good in benefit-cost estimation.[32] (The study carried forward general efforts in the Bank to develop methods for analyzing the results of social projects.[33]) The social demand function was used in an empirical analysis in 1980 and in quantifying the benefits of the planned food supplementation portion of the Tamil Nadu project.[34]

A 1981 study developed a conceptual framework for estimating nutrition effects of agricultural and rural development projects and policies.[35] It suggested that, when a tradeoff exists between nutrition and other economic benefits of a project, modifications be made to meet nutrition goals only if the cost of doing so is less than the cost of achieving the same goals by the most cost-effective alternative. This use of marginal cost-effectiveness to determine the extent to which nutrition concerns should be incorporated in the design of agricultural projects was elaborated in a 1983 study.[36]

One study went beyond conventional approaches in estimating demand functions for calories for a set of developing countries. The estimates were based on the theory of characteristic demand,[37] which measures utility to consumers by the characteristics of food. This allowed caloric intake distribution to be estimated directly from income distribution data. A study of food consumption in Indonesia used data from a national household expenditure survey to estimate the elasticity of demand for food, with respect to income and price.[38] Expenditure and household consumption surveys for Brazil, the cities of Bogotá and Cali in Colombia, the Terai region of Nepal, and East Java in Indonesia have been analyzed for their nutrition implications, as have food balance sheets for China. A new analytic survey tool developed by World Bank staff, the Living Standards Measurement Study, devotes prominent attention to nutrition status and its determinants. Taking advantage of advanced computer and survey techniques, the approach serves as an early warning system, making it possible to provide reports to country officials within two months of when household and community data are collected. Such surveys have been completed in Côte d'Ivoire and Peru, and similar ones are scheduled for several other countries in Sub-Saharan Africa.[39]

Measuring Nutrition Effects

To help resolve the issue of how to measure nutrition effects, a review of various indicators that might be appropriate for household surveys in developing countries discussed advantages and limitations of each.[40] Bank researchers have also examined various ways of gauging the magnitude of energy deficits. In the Tamil Nadu nutrition project, for instance, their comparisons suggested that simply monitoring weight gain was a cost-effective means of measuring changes in nutrition status. The probability analysis that was employed in these determinations—from knowing the time of day to weigh a child most accurately to reducing the chance of bypassing a malnourished child—has advanced the methodology of growth monitoring and direct feeding programs. The "growth velocity" measure has proved valuable in educating parents, for it increases their awareness of the nutrition needs of very young children and provides an easily understood signal that a faltering child needs special attention.

If adequate weight gain is adopted as the indicator of a child's health, precision in measuring and recording weight becomes all the more critical. Since in, say, five-year-olds, a weight gain or loss of even 200 grams can be important, growth charts need intervals that make plotting and detecting small changes easy. In response to this need, the Bank has been involved in developing a new-style growth chart that both improves accuracy in plotting and helps health workers and parents see whether the weight gain has been adequate.[41]

Another Bank staff member successfully developed and tested a new version of a tape to measure arm circumference as an indicator of nutrition status.[42] The "Echeverri tape" has been used in Bank-assisted projects in Bolivia, Ecuador, Paraguay, and Peru. Several studies of household behavior have provided useful guidelines for predicting how households will react to changes in food prices, incomes, demands on women's time, and the like.[43]

Beyond the Bank

The interaction of the World Bank with the scientific research community has helped to shape the Bank's priorities and projects and has contributed to the general store of knowledge on nutrition. The Bank, for example, has helped fund nutrition studies at the International Food Policy Research Institute (IFPRI), at the same time gaining access to its research funded by other sources. A recent non-Bank funded IFPRI study on Kenya has contributed to Bank thinking, for instance, by confirming empirically that increased income alone does not necessarily improve nutrition.[44]

Bank staff have participated in the National Academy of Sciences' World Food and Nutrition Study and Working Group on Food Aid.[45] The Bank also played an active role in organizing an interagency research program for the United Nations Sub-Committee on Nutrition and for this program sponsored studies on nutrition education, nutrition and child survival, and nutrition effects of policies encouraging cash crops over subsistence crops.[46]

IN SUM, the nutrition research undertaken or financed by the Bank in recent years has on balance been useful in recommending policy and shaping operations. It has helped provide information on the nature and causes of malnutrition, ways to estimate social benefits and costs, insight into the characteristics of effective food supplementation projects, understanding of the design and targeting of consumer-oriented food price subsidies, and guidelines for integrating nutrition objectives into the design of other development projects. Future work can be less wide-ranging, focusing on specific problems linked to implementation of nutrition activities.

7 | What Has Been Learned?

WHEN THE WORLD BANK began its discussions on nutrition there was some uncertainty among its Executive Directors about whether malnutrition was a development problem and whether there were things that could be done about it that the Bank was suited to do. The results of some seventy-five pieces of research and other analytic work show that the problem merits attention as a development issue, and operational experience has demonstrated that nutrition projects such as those assisted by the Bank can contribute to a solution.

The first two Bank-aided projects, those in Brazil and Indonesia, began slowly and had serious difficulties, but finished strong. Most of their targets were met, as were those of the third project, in Colombia. The fourth project, begun in Tamil Nadu, India, in 1980 and built on the earlier experience, met all of its performance objectives. In number of people who benefited, physical structures completed, and other commonly used indicators, the four projects were very successful. In delivery of services, most of the components met their targets, and overall an estimated 3.6 million people benefited from the projects—46 percent more than the original estimates in Bank appraisal reports.

The efforts appear to have penetrated more deeply in the poorest segments of the population than most Bank-assisted projects. And proportionately more women were involved, both as administrators and as beneficiaries. (The important role of women at every level—as top project directors, instructors, community nutrition workers, members of the women's working groups, and, of course, the clients themselves—is a striking aspect of the Tamil Nadu project. It is unlikely that women have been involved as extensively in any other project in which the Bank has been involved.)

Policy impact, as measured by government resources committed

94

and policies and programs changed, was substantial in several cases. Less than had been hoped was learned about the nutrition impact of the projects, although some useful data emerged. Despite the uneven quality of the evaluations, taken together they represent a fairly consistent picture of measurable effects. In short, following rocky beginnings, the nutrition projects made a creditable showing.

The Operation of the Projects

Much experience has been gained on operational aspects of project design and management. Such lessons—regarding what can and cannot be done—might be profitably applied to future work in nutrition; some have applicability in other sectors.

Implementation

The interventions that worked most smoothly were the delivery of nutrition services in Tamil Nadu, nutrition education in Indonesia, preschool feeding and stimulation (PROAPE) in Brazil, anemia control in Indonesia, and the food subsidy and marketing efficiency programs (PINS, especially in the form of its modified successor, PROAB, and Rede Somar) in Brazil. The efforts that were most difficult to implement and for which there is least to show were those that tried to build nutrition considerations into agricultural planning in Brazil and Indonesia. In general, institution-building efforts, particularly those intended to build capacity for monitoring and evaluation, fell short of expectation.

Costs

Costs of programs varied dramatically, from Brazil's self-supporting food marketing program (Rede Somar) and Indonesia's very low-cost nutrition education effort at one end of the spectrum to the consumer food subsidy programs at the other. Those components that would, if expanded on a national scale, consume less than 2 percent of the national budget are the Indonesian nutrition education and NIPP programs, the Brazilian PINS program targeted at urban areas, the Colombian consumer food subsidy program targeted for poor regions of the country, and, of course, the self-supporting Brazilian food marketing program; the Tamil Nadu nutrition services would come close, at just over 2 percent. At 1 percent of the national budget, the two Indonesian programs and Brazil's food marketing program would be viable; the Brazilian and Colombian subsidy programs would not.

It is not possible to say that one Bank-assisted program was less expensive than another for the benefits received, largely because the programs did not share objectives. Some, nonetheless, particularly the Indonesian nutrition education component and the Tamil Nadu project, appear to have been more cost-effective than other interventions on which governments already have spent large amounts. Thus great opportunities exist for efforts intended to increase efficiencies.

Targeting

The projects were able to reach more people with better nutrition services more efficiently (at a more acceptable cost) than most earlier programs. Increases in effectiveness and efficiency can largely be attributed to some mix of targeting—by area, age, income, or other criterion, such as providing subsidies during those months when food prices are highest. The conclusion that emerges repeatedly is that appropriate targeting techniques can lower substantially the financial and administrative costs of consumer programs and increase their nutrition effects.

In Brazil's revised consumer food subsidy program and Colombia's food coupon program, geographic targeting pinpointed the lowest-income areas. This proved to be more effective in identifying those in need and less of an administrative burden than eligibility requirements based on household income. It also allowed subsidized foods to be available routinely, an important consideration for low-income people who generally buy in small quantities. In Colombia, further targeting allowed benefits to accrue disproportionately to pregnant or nursing women and young children. The Brazil PROAPE program and the Tamil Nadu nutrition services targeted by both area and age. In Tamil Nadu, children were targeted for assistance during the nutritionally most important two and one-half years of their lives; this represented the most tightly targeted of the Bank-supported efforts, while maintaining a competitive cost per beneficiary for a feeding program.

One type of income targeting that gets around the need for means tests is targeting by food type. The best foods to subsidize are those that are consumed predominantly by the poor and have little appeal to others. Coarse grains, such as sorghum and millet, processed cassava flour, and certain legumes favored by the poor—macassar beans in Brazil, for example, lentils in central India, and black gram in south India—meet these criteria. These foods are generally consumed in small quantities, if at all, by persons at middle- and upper-income levels, so subsidies would benefit the poor disproportionately. (The subsidized price should not be set so low that there is danger of diversion to animal feed or exports.) Such commodity targeting may be particularly appropriate in connection with structural adjustment lending programs and (as described in chapter 8) is part of a plan to help the government of Morocco invest more wisely in nutrition. Although overly refined targeting can raise administrative costs, these experiences show that ways can be found to target without incurring untenable costs and bureaucratic burdens.[a]

Project Design

The main lessons concerning the design of nutrition projects (like those in other sectors in their early operations) are to limit the number of components and the complexity of administration. The multiplicity of possible actions should not be allowed to dictate complex projects. Analysis to define the content of a project should be fairly broad, but the resulting project should not be expected to address all the factors that affect nutrition status. Everything relates to everything else, but not equally. Actions should be sharply focused on a few critical needs, recognizing that these sometimes must cut across sectors. Nutrition projects should be viewed as part of a constellation of development actions either planned or already under way in a country.

No single set of interventions can be prescribed for nutrition projects, given the vast differences among countries. Nonetheless,

a. Perfect targeting is rarely practical or even desirable on cost-effectiveness grounds. Per Pinstrup-Andersen points out that individuals within households should be targeted only in cases of serious nutritional deficiencies (as in Tamil Nadu). Otherwise, households should be targeted to receive subsidies or food-linked income transfers. See Per Pinstrup-Andersen, "Assuring Food Security and Adequate Nutrition for the Poor during Periods of Economic Crisis and Macroeconomic Adjustments: Policy Options and Experience with Food Subsidies and Transfer Programs," paper prepared for the Second Takemi Symposium on International Health, Harvard University, Cambridge, Mass., May 1986.

common guidance can be provided from the experience on what to search for in analysis and on the types of measures for best addressing different types and causes of malnutrition under various circumstances. Given shifting economic conditions and the fast pace of change in the nutrition field, projects must be flexible enough to respond to and take advantage of unexpected situations.

Duration

The first nutrition projects in a country should probably run for at least six years, if demonstrated improvement in the nutrition status of large population groups is an expected outcome. Some of the components of the early projects lasted such a short time that it was impossible to measure their impact on nutrition status or learn a great deal from the experience. It should not have been a surprise that governments need time to get services running smoothly, particularly when projects require a new philosophy, a new design concept, a new delivery system, a new organization, and new staff. And more is now known than at the outset about the time and difficulties involved in generating reliable data. Studies by the Bank's Operations Evaluation Department indicate that during the same period projects in other sectors have had much the same experience.

Performance

The nutrition projects generally stack up well against Bank projects in other sectors, particularly first projects. They have outperformed or equaled the average Bank project in their accuracy of cost estimates,[b] adherence to project completion schedules, compliance with loan conditions, and procurement schedules and have done less well in speed of disbursements, performance of management, and thoroughness of reporting.[c] They have generally performed better than the first four projects in other sectors or first projects in other sectors in the countries with nutrition projects. Furthermore, the performance of the nutrition projects has improved over time: preparation

b. The only cost overrun of the four, 26 percent in Colombia, was nearly all the result of expansion of activities from what originally was envisioned.

c. Based on a Bankwide system of quantitative indicators to rank the progress of projects.

and supervision of the fourth project were considerably more efficient than that of the first.

Applications in Other Sectors

In several instances, lessons learned in the nutrition projects, research, and sector work can be applied to strengthen work in other sectors. The social marketing approaches for nutrition education in Indonesia, already adopted under other funding auspices for national programs in the Dominican Republic, Ecuador, and Swaziland, would be useful for health and family planning education.[1] The training and supervision concepts employed in Tamil Nadu are among several features of that project that are applicable to most rural projects.[2] Brazil's PROAPE experience, which invested in the nutrition of the very young to get a later higher return on investments in the school system, has implications for education projects.[3] The targeting techniques developed in the nutrition projects may be useful to several sectors, as they may be for the policy-based lending of structural and sectoral adjustment programs that are described in chapter 8.

The Impact of the Projects

What can be said about the difference these projects have made? Two types of effects can be discerned. The more direct of the two is the impacts on the nutrition status of beneficiaries that project evaluations were able to show. The second type relates to the effect projects may have had on the way borrowing countries perceive nutrition and act on that perception in devising policies and programs. Although nutrition improvement is surely the goal of policies and programs, changes in the way governments view and act on nutrition also are significant in that they determine the sustainability of the efforts started by the projects.

Nutrition Status

The most striking impact was in Tamil Nadu, where serious and severe malnutrition was 40 percent less common among thirteen- to thirty-six-month-old children in project villages than in baseline control villages and might have been better still, had the children been enrolled earlier. The significant 1.75 kilogram weight advantage was maintained at age five, two years after the children completed the program. Similar positive findings resulted from comparisons with neighboring programs. Among all six- to sixty-month-old children who in 1986 were in or had graduated from TINP, serious and severe malnutrition was down 53 percent—to a rate (8 percent) roughly half that of children in nonproject areas.

Successfully conducted evaluations also demonstrated improvement in nutrition status because of the nutrition education program in the Indonesia project. The number of moderately and severely malnourished children in the program group was half that of comparable villages with other nutrition education efforts, and 40 percent of the children were growing more rapidly. The mean weight of project children in their second year of life was a significant one-half to one kilogram heavier.

In the sanitation program in Colombia, nutrition problems were reduced by 15 percent for every 10 percent increase in households with latrines. Results look promising but more needs to be known about the anemia control program in Indonesia and the marketing interventions (PINS-PROAB and Rede Somar) in Brazil. The gardens components in Colombia and Indonesia increased production, but neither their evaluations nor that of nutrition efforts built on agricultural extension in Brazil were capable of detecting any nutrition effect.

Beyond these operations, not as much was learned about impact on nutrition status as was initially hoped, largely because expectations of what could be learned during the time frame in an operational (rather than research) setting were overly ambitious. Several of the evaluations were sufficiently flawed—either methodologically or in execution—that they could not stand up in scientific court. Even these evaluations, however, may be instructive when reviewed together because of the common directions in which they point. (Further limitations to the evaluation of impact of nutrition projects are described in chapter 8.)

National Policies and Programs

More has been learned about the impact on policies and programs. Projects have affected development plans and programs of some of the borrowing countries and have demonstrated what can be achieved in countries that have at least a modicum of commitment in this area. Something also has been learned about how government policies are shaped during the preparation of a loan and about how the investments can be used to bring nutrition issues to the attention of the policymakers.

In its 1986 annual review of project performance, the Bank's Operations Evaluation Department credited the nutrition projects with making important contributions toward the development of a new sector in participating countries. Where substantial national nutrition improvement efforts are already under way, as in India and Indonesia, the Bank-assisted projects offer an opportunity to experiment with new concepts (new approaches to nutrition education, for instance) and refine techniques (for training and supervision, for example) that can then be incorporated into national programs to increase their cost-effectiveness.

Some of the Bank-assisted nutrition activities have been expanded, even to a national scale, and some have been taken up or are being planned in other countries. In Brazil, PROAPE, which began in a single state, was planned for extension at government expense to every state and territory; Colombia and Mexico are planning similar efforts, and other Latin American countries have shown interest. Brazil's consumer food subsidy program has been broadened (with modifications made as a result of the initial evaluation) from an experiment in Recife to five cities and 1.2 million participants, and the budget has increased more than tenfold. The Rede Somar program has been replicated in three other Bank projects and served as the model for a large Bank-assisted program in Colombia. The Colombian food coupon program was a prime casualty of that country's austerity drive in the early 1980s, but the government elected in 1986 appointed a presidential task force to consider its lessons and the possibility of reviving the disbanded program as part of a new food and nutrition plan. Meanwhile, the nutrition-oriented health component of the Colombia nutrition project helped a fledgling primary health care program come into its own to the point that it is now a national program.

The short-term, seasonal credit (CAP) introduced to very poor farmers in the Bank-assisted nutrition project in Sergipe has subsequently been incorporated in seven of the ten Bank-assisted rural development projects in Brazil's Northeast, and social extension agents in fifteen Bank-assisted rural extension programs in Brazil now perform nutrition services introduced in the Sergipe component. The Sergipe model has become an integral part of the thinking of the Brazilian rural extension agency. And the Sergipe evaluation contributed to the World Bank's decision to include land purchase in rural development projects.

In Indonesia most of the elements tested in combination for the first time in the Nutrition Intervention Pilot Project (growth monitoring, treatment of diarrhea, nutrition education, immunization, supplementary feeding, and family planning) have become standard features of the national program that is the main component of a follow-on Bank-assisted nutrition and community health project. The principles and approaches of the nutrition education component have been incorporated into a program that covered 30,000 villages in 1983 and was expected to double in the following five years. Gardens have become a part of the Bank-assisted third agricultural extension project, and the government has adopted the NIPP concept of using "village laboratories" to test new program ideas. The Ministry of Health has adopted the project's supplementary feeding approach as the standard for all government-assisted village feeding efforts.

Because the Tamil Nadu project began later than the others and in 1987 was still being implemented, its long-term impact on policies and programs is yet to be felt. Nonetheless, the innovative training and supervision techniques that were critical to the success of that project are already being put to good use to improve Tamil Nadu's large Integrated Child Development Scheme.

The four governments that sponsored the original large-scale nutrition projects are making unprecedented budgetary commitments for nutrition actions. They provided 64 percent of the quarter of a billion dollars needed for the four projects and borrowed the rest. They also spent considerably more than that for nutrition, albeit not always effectively, and in some cases were able to avoid still larger expenditures by deciding against actions that project experience showed to be of questionable value. In three of the four countries second nutrition projects have been requested (one of which began in 1986), and in the fourth a health project that includes nutrition was made possible by groundwork laid by the first nutrition project.

A request for a follow-on project, of course, does not necessarily reflect satisfaction with the performance of the first. But it does show political will to invest in nutrition. A number of other countries also have expressed interest in Bank-assisted nutrition projects. Clearly some governments are ready to commit substantial resources to nutrition.

8 | The Years Ahead

CURRENT decisionmaking on nutrition programs is undertaken in an environment that has changed markedly over a decade. A surge of conservative politics, particularly among donor countries, and a more hostile international economic environment have endangered the opportunities created in the 1970s to address basic human needs. Distributional issues no longer receive the priority they commanded just a few years ago. Untenable external debt, balance of payments problems, and budgetary crises have diverted attention to production of export crops and have brought about cuts in social programs, generally without much consideration of the nutrition consequences.

The international development community that for a good part of the 1970s was active in pursuing the alleviation of poverty has shifted energies to structural adjustment, calling for fundamental economic reforms by governments to reduce fiscal and trade deficits. Granted that such adjustments often are necessities, the challenge is to do them in a way that, at a minimum, will not disproportionately affect the poor and, ideally, will benefit the most vulnerable groups. The malnourished are the least able to absorb economic adversity; even in good times they exist on the slimmest of margins. The food consumption of the poorest must be prevented from getting worse. (Issues and options for ensuring that all people have access to enough food to lead active and healthy lives have been explored in a recent World Bank policy study on food security.[1])

Furthermore, there are several indications that conditions are worsening in many nations. World Bank analysis of thirty countries has found that, during the first half of the 1980s, all but three experienced declines in per capita calorie consumption. Increases in incidence of malnutrition and deaths from it have been observed in several Sub-Saharan African countries. And absolute poverty and malnutrition are on the increase in Latin America. In Brazil's Northeast, infant mortality appears to have increased by 25 percent during 1982–84.[2]

In this grim environment, political commitment is the first prerequisite to solving the problem of malnutrition. Governments committed to alleviating malnutrition can make dramatic progress, and as they gain experience with nutrition interventions, progress can breed progress. In countries that lack commitment at the top level of government, groups committed to nutrition often can be identified and strengthened, ready to move forward when the policy environment changes.

Malnutrition is intrinsically a local problem, affecting the individual, the family, and the community. Thus local effort and resources must be mobilized to increase people's own capacity to fight malnutrition, as witnessed in the Indonesian and Thai experiences. Communities clearly are better able to understand their problems than are outsiders, and they almost always have untapped resources. Empowering communities to become more self-reliant is not easy, and less so in some cultures than others, but is worth the effort: local solutions are less exposed to the vagaries of outside political winds and economic forces over which they have no control.

For all the difficulties that have been experienced, efforts to institutionalize nutrition objectives within the health and agricultural sectors must continue. Improvements in nutrition must become an integral part of the missions and methods of these sectors. Basic changes need to be made in the way personnel in these fields are trained and rewarded, to enhance their appreciation of the consequences of their work. Nutrition considerations must be integrated into the curricula in the fields of agricultural economics and extension, medicine, and public health. And government workers in these fields must be evaluated at least partly on their contribution to nutrition.

Malnutrition, however, is a systemic phenomenon, and care must be exercised that a piecemeal approach does not supplant this vision. Concern must be strong enough at the highest political and planning levels to ensure that nutrition efforts within sectors are not neglected or diluted and that the efforts of various government, private, and foreign assistance organizations are coordinated. This coordination generally will require some kind of organizational focal point.

One important area where national attention must in a broad way be directed to nutrition is in the context of economic adjustment, as an example below from Morocco illustrates.

The Role of Nutrition in Policy-Based Lending

In 1985 the government of Morocco was in a financial bind, with a fiscal deficit of 11 percent of its gross domestic product. To help reduce public expenditures, the International Monetary Fund proposed, as part of a stabilization program, a phasing out of consumer food subsidies, which accounted for $400 million, or nearly 12 percent of Morocco's budget.

How would this affect the poor who already were living on the margin? Analysis found that although a disproportionately small share of the subsidy—16 percent—reached the poorest three-tenths of the population, this amount nonetheless represented a significant part of their inadequate diets. Elimination of subsidies on only three staples—wheat, cooking oil, and sugar—would reduce by 20 percent the real incomes of those considered to be at nutritional risk. The Bank proposed a program that would compensate the poor for the decline in consumer food subsidies.

First, taking steps to lower producer costs would help reduce the market price of basic foods, particularly sugar. Second, barley and maize, which are consumed primarily by lower-income groups, would be blended with wheat to lower the market price of processed grain and, if tests showed it to be required, would be subsidized. Third, the scope and coverage of feeding programs directed to poor mothers, infants, children, and others at nutritional risk would be increased. Such a reformulation was projected to improve nutrition at one-fifth the cost of the earlier subsidy program. There would also be an annual savings of nearly $200 million in foreign exchange.

Opportunities for Reform

Morocco is one of several countries that are currently, with Bank support, planning similar nutrition-related actions to protect the poor. The actions complement a relatively new approach to development assistance—policy-based lending. This approach contrasts with conventional Bank operations that lend for investments in specific projects. Through policy-based lending countries facing serious debt-servicing and balance of payments difficulties are eligible to obtain loans or credits to help them implement reforms needed for growth and to relieve such pressures in the future. Reform measures typically involve reducing public expenditures, changing trade and exchange rate policy, and enacting institutional reforms, all of which can have a direct or indirect effect on the real income of households and so their ability to acquire food and nutrition services. In such a setting, nutrition usually looms large.

The reforms should, in theory, benefit the entire population in the long run by increasing economic growth. But they could well have nutritionally negative repercussions on the poor in the short and medium terms, unless they are properly planned. Research has shown that the negative effects could happen through shifts in house-hold income and purchasing power—and, by extension, nutrition—brought on by changes in prices, wages, or employment, or by changes in government expenditures on programs aimed at the poor.[3] A given policy change will affect groups differently, depending on whether they are net producers or net consumers of food. For example, a rise in producer prices should increase the incomes of farmers but reduce the purchasing power of wage laborers.

The dilemma is how to encourage adjustments for long-term growth and development while protecting those groups already in nutritionally precarious positions before adjustment. In this connection the targeting lessons of Bank nutrition projects can help in de-signing programs that enhance food security for the poor or at least cushion them from the shock of adjustment.

Not all the compensatory measures that flow from the analysis need be incorporated within a structural adjustment loan or credit itself. Actions can be undertaken through more conventional nutri-tion or health projects (see below). And sectoral adjustment loans—an increasingly common type of policy-based lending—in other areas, chiefly agriculture, can take account of the implications for nutrition of proposed actions and thus increase the likelihood of food security for the poor. All adjustment lending programs should monitor vul-nerable groups to give early warning of adverse social effects.[a]

a. Since structural adjustment loans commonly are made as a series of quick-disbursing loans, early warning can be achieved by building into the first loan a pro-vision for data collection, such as a household expenditure survey. When data indicate

Consumer Food Subsidies

Because of their importance to nutrition and their frequent consideration for reform in adjustment programs, consumer food subsidies, a hotly debated topic, merit further discussion. The high fiscal costs of explicit subsidy programs tempt governments either to set low prices for domestically produced food or to rely excessively on foreign food aid. Both policies discourage local agricultural production. Some subsidies are difficult to administer, and any subsidy once in place is difficult to cut because it builds up political constituencies.

But research and sector work show that few other nutrition interventions offer the possibility of substantially and reasonably quickly alleviating the widespread malnutrition and reducing the nutrition-related deaths among poor people in developing countries. In several countries subsidy programs have helped significantly to increase food consumption by poor households and appear to have reduced malnutrition, especially among children. Moreover, the financial problems associated with such programs can be reduced if the programs are carefully targeted.[4] Effectively reaching the rural poor with such programs unfortunately remains a problem.

Consumer food subsidy programs also often provide a politically palatable instrument of policy to governments whose objectives include reducing the level of absolute poverty. Those governments might in principle be able to achieve their objective by redistributing financial assets or income, perhaps in some cases more efficiently than by subsidizing food. Political and fiscal realities in most countries, however, sharply curtail that possibility. The broad appeal of alleviating hunger makes consumer food subsidies politically more acceptable.[b]

Country-specific analysis will indicate whether, in the context of broad pricing and equity issues and development needs, subsidies

---

that compensatory measures are warranted, subsequent loans can address these issues. Because policies can affect groups differently, the data would have to be disaggregated to consider each group at risk.

b. Furthermore, such nutrition-type social sector actions have been judged to be "less likely to arouse elite opposition than projects meant to assist the agricultural production of the poor," and "their benefits, moreover, may be less readily appropriable by elites." See Judith Tendler, *Rural Projects through Urban Eyes: An Interpretation of the World Bank's New-Style Rural Development Projects*, World Bank Staff Working Paper 532 (Washington, D.C., 1982).

are sensible (that is, could be set in place without adverse effects on agricultural production and with feasible financial and administrative costs) as part of a strategy to deal with malnutrition. Special attention needs to be given to how such programs can be made cost-effective and how their potentially adverse effects can be minimized.

Nutrition Projects and Components

The vast number of people suffering from malnutrition and the prospect that better nutrition can contribute to the development of human capital and to the reduction of fertility have convinced the World Bank's management that malnutrition is an important development problem, and one the institution should address. If the Bank is to make more than a peripheral contribution to nutrition, it sometimes must support projects directed primarily at nutrition goals.

Experience has shown that nutrition projects focus attention on malnutrition and attack it in ways that other Bank operations have not been able to. In contrast, nutrition components of projects in other sectors generally have not commanded enough attention from either governments or lending institutions to make a consequential difference. Nor are projects in other sectors (health being the main exception) necessarily located in the geographic areas or directed at the particular groups in which nutrition problems are greatest.

Unquestionably, the primary health care system should be used, whenever possible, to introduce nutrition services. But the present scope, coverage, and fragility of most health systems limit their ability to attack malnutrition comprehensively. The deteriorating financial situation in many countries in recent years, with gravest consequences for the food consumption and nutrition levels of the poor, has made it even harder for health facilities to meet nutrition needs. Dependence on the health system alone to fill the needs is likely to create disillusionment and to risk neglect of actions in other areas.

The nutrition projects have proved viable, and they have demonstrated the power to inform policymakers, help mobilize constituencies, catalyze other nutrition actions, and institutionalize project objectives in ways that lead to much larger programs. The projects have been small in relation to the problems they have attacked, but they have been able to help set change in motion.

Although the operational lessons, good and bad, from the Bank's experience are stressed here, the most important contribution of the nutrition projects appears to have been their effect on the priority, commitment, policy and program choices, and level of country support for nutrition actions. Because nutrition is a relatively new field, Bank-assisted projects in nutrition have probably had greater impact than some projects in more established sectors, where well-formed policies and programs already existed.

Despite the substantial expenditures that a number of countries have for some time been making on programs that affect nutrition, there is commonly room for improvement in how that money is used. In Brazil direct and indirect costs for nutrition were estimated at $3 billion in 1986, with considerable increases projected for 1987–89. About one-third was for a subsidy program for wheat, which benefits high-income groups as well as low-income groups. Much of the rest of the $3 billion was for programs to feed industrial workers and school children, questionable *nutrition* priorities for Brazil. (If an amount equal to the costs incurred by Brazil for nutrition in 1986 could be redirected in some program form to only the neediest fifth of the population, that amount would constitute a hypothetical transfer equal to 45 percent of their cash income.) Similarly Tamil Nadu, in addition to the Bank-assisted project, is spending $300 million a year—which approaches 15 percent of the state budget—on a program for midday meals for children that is not finely targeted. A main purpose of Bank-supported nutrition projects should be to help governments increase the efficiency of existing programs. This need is especially great during the present period of stabilization and structural adjustment. As many countries face external pressures to cut consumer food subsidies and other social programs (and have their own worries about where to cut the budget), the Bank, through a nutrition project, may help governments identify cuts that make nutrition sense—or at least avoid nutrition damage.

Nutrition projects are likely to be the best way to deal with nutrition issues that do not fall in the exclusive domain of either agriculture or health ministries or to seize opportunities to work with, say, social welfare ministries or marketing bodies. In some circumstances a nutrition project may be appropriate because the nutrition system is more fully developed than the health system (as was the case in Indonesia), or because adding nutrition would overly complicate management of a health project, or because enlarging government's interest in and capacity to deal with nutrition is a main purpose of the project.

Are Nutrition Projects Replicable?

The four projects have demonstrated that certain nutrition actions, within the settings tried, are technically feasible, cost-effective, and affordable. Whether they can be mounted and effectively administered on a larger scale in those countries depends most of all on the existing infrastructure. Prospects would be good for expanding the food marketing interventions and the food delivery part of the preschool program in Brazil, for example, which are looked after largely by an experienced food marketing agency (COBAL). In the Tamil Nadu project and the nutrition education program in Indonesia, prospects also would be promising.

Can lessons learned be applied in other, less experienced places? Several of the approaches developed in the four projects would be applicable for most all countries (including industrial countries)—the new-style nutrition education pioneered in Indonesia, for instance, and the supervision and training concepts fostered in Tamil Nadu. Clearly, some of the more successful efforts (in Indonesia, for instance, NIPP in Bojonegoro) depended on unusual local activism; tighter and more expensive Tamil Nadu–type management systems may be needed to replicate and sustain such programs in areas of less commitment. The limitations to absorbing external assistance in some countries, particularly in Sub-Saharan Africa, also pose special problems. Nonetheless, the type of analysis that led to the development of new projects and the principles that underlay the interventions generally are transferable, even though the specifics of a program will depend on the particular characteristics of the country (such as the availability of financial resources, the sophistication of staff, the monetization of the society, and the extent of urbanization, referral systems, and infrastructure). Interventions that introduce simple technologies are most easily transferable, provided the basic conditions (centralized processing for adding nutrients to staples, for example) are met.

The Institutional Links for Nutrition Work

There is no obvious governmental institutional framework for nutrition. It may fit into a country's health, agriculture, social welfare, or, under special circumstances, planning ministry. In the early years of the Colombia project, working through the planning department held out the most promise (though the suprasectoral approach could not be maintained later in the project), while in Tamil Nadu an interagency structure proved to be successful. The appropriate institution will differ from country to country. Appointment of a top-level advocate can help muster the necessary political, financial, and technical resources.

Whether nutrition services should be integrated with other services in the field or operated separately so as to concentrate on fewer actions depends on preference and the situation in the individual country. Conventional thinking about health calls for totally integrated services; the Tamil Nadu experience indicates that a less than fully integrated but coordinated approach can be workable. Although full integration of services will, more often than not, be the goal, there is no apparent reason to assume that a separate nutrition cadre is not warranted in some instances.

The Evaluation of Impact

Measuring the impact and economic benefits of human resource projects is generally difficult, and measuring the effects of nutrition projects is more difficult than most. The problem is especially great for development agencies and governments accustomed to basing their decisions on engineering criteria and financial analyses.

Because nutrition is a relatively new field of study still full of unknowns, the measurements currently being used may not always be focused on the right thing. For instance, recent evidence suggests that energy consumption that does not show up in growth is used in increased physical activity; if so, the measures used in evaluating nutrition projects probably have not captured a good portion of the benefits derived. Lower levels of physical activity are now seen as an accommodation to lower energy intake. In children accommodation may also be reflected in slower cognitive and affective development, even though physical development may not be noticeably influenced. Where such accommodations to lower energy intake are pervasive in a society, the reduced levels of performance may be mistakenly interpreted as the norm. (Changes in growth patterns can be expected from programs for the severely malnourished, as in Tamil Nadu, but not necessarily from those for the moderately malnourished, who are a much larger part of the population and are therefore likely to have a greater effect on overall economic activity.)

Just as all short-run effects may not be known within the lifetime of certain components of a nutrition project, the long-run, even inter-generational effects of malnutrition clearly will not be known until well after the conclusion of the projects. (Mothers of short stature because of chronic childhood malnutrition are more likely to have small babies who in turn are more likely to be malnourished or to die young.) The policymaker is thus faced with three choices: conclude there is only modest benefit from such programs (that is, the benefits are limited to those that can be demonstrated by anthropometric evaluations of growth, which in cases of mild and moderate malnutrition may not show much change); withhold final judgment on investments in nutrition until perhaps the mid-1990s when better measurement tools may be available; or accept the common sense analysis that the malnourished will benefit if nutrition is provided.

The choice obviously should be the third option. That economic effects of nutrition interventions cannot be measured with the precision claimed in some other sectors does not deny the significance of the malnutrition problem or diminish the reality that malnutrition contributes greatly to many of the diseases that developing countries are devoting substantial resources to eradicate. In spite of the uncertainty in measuring the results of nutrition operations, some governments appear ready to make substantial program and policy commitments to nutrition. Those programs must be carefully designed and monitored, so that they can employ the most cost-effective, affordable means of bringing about changes in behavior and food consumption, with the likelihood that such actions will lead to better nutrition.

Priority Actions

The World Bank's research and sector work suggest that certain strategies for improving nutrition merit high priority in most countries. Particularly important are strategies to accelerate growth in the income of the poor and, in many circumstances, in food production (especially those in which producer and needy consumer are the same, as in Sub-Saharan Africa). These approaches, already being major aims of the Bank, do not require special attention in the context of Bank-assisted nutrition work. Attention must be given, however, to helping low-income groups bridge the gap until their incomes and education bring their food consumption levels and nutrition practices up to their nutritional needs and to helping those outside the mainstream of national growth.

In policy discussions with governments and in the orientation of projects in other sectors, particularly agriculture, the Bank has the opportunity to raise nutrition and food consumption issues. Efforts have been made to inject such issues in economic and agricultural sector analyses, to encourage consideration of agriculture projects in which food consumption for the poor is an objective, and to introduce nutrition content into agriculture projects that have potentially negative effects (particularly those that encourage semisubsistence farmers to grow cash crops). Only modest gains have been made along these lines. The failure to emphasize or institutionalize nutrition elements reflects the mistaken perceptions that nutrition problems are primarily food production problems or that they are by-products of inadequate economic growth and cannot be acted on directly.

Useful work on nutrition can also be done through health and population projects, even recognizing current limitations of scale and scope. As recent evidence suggests that underlying malnutrition accounts for much of the difference among health interventions in impact on child survival, the objectives of health projects will be difficult to achieve if nutrition status is not improved.[5] And projects to reduce population growth are linked with improved nutrition.[6]

In some instances, however, labeling actions as nutrition is an important means of raising issues; a health or population project is a poor vehicle for examining food distribution policy or raising nutrition-related agricultural issues. Nutrition projects may be the best way to deal with intersectoral issues or to harness political commitment and public concern.

Nutrition Projects

Future nutrition projects can be more narrowly focused and simply designed than the early undertakings, now that concepts have been clarified and interventions operationalized. Project experience and the analysis of those projects have pointed up areas where improvements in nutrition can be made and areas where little is likely to be accomplished.

New projects are apt to realize the rewards of this learning-by-doing exercise. This already is markedly evident in Tamil Nadu, the first of the Bank's second-generation projects. The Bank should now be prepared to lend in appropriate countries for three types of nutrition projects: those that are intended to alleviate the most critical short-term nutritional needs (Tamil Nadu–type projects); those that improve food distribution, make government expenditure on food and the food marketing system more efficient, and otherwise strengthen the family food basket (this type of project may be particularly appropriate for countries undergoing structural adjustment); and those that fortify food staples with vitamins and minerals or provide these micronutrients through supplementation programs. As borrowers develop new projects, they should be encouraged to consider reshaping their current expenditures for nutrition.

Future nutrition projects should be directed at reducing infant and child morbidity and mortality, promoting child growth, and improving human capital. In the future, support can most profitably be concentrated on projects to combat energy-protein malnutrition and the diseases and handicaps caused by deficiencies of vitamin A, iodine, and iron. These types of malnutrition are widespread and their consequences severe.[c] And they can be treated if trained people, funds, and political commitment are available.

The three project models can help. First, where advanced malnutrition is prevalent among the very young (and among expectant or nursing women), the Tamil Nadu model offers a cost-effective means of identifying the nutritionally needy and helping them through food supplements for a limited period. The concept—providing food almost as medicine—may be particularly useful for countries that are self-sufficient in basic foods and for countries that receive substantial amounts of food aid, so that the aid is efficiently targeted to those in greatest need.

Maternal supplementation along the lines developed in Tamil Nadu looks to be one of the best means of reducing child mortality and improving the nutritional status of those who survive, as well as protecting the health of the mother, which is also essential for child health and survival. Researchers in Guatemala and India have found that supplementing the diets of undernourished pregnant women significantly reduces stillbirths and infant deaths in the first month after birth and improves birth weight.

c. Other nutrient deficiencies can have serious consequences but are much less prevalent (for example, rickets from vitamin D deficiency) or have less serious consequences even though they are widespread (for example, flouride deficiency).

Second, when concern extends to all members of the family and to broader distributional issues, assistance should be designed to enlarge the family food basket (without waiting for economic development), particularly during periods of seasonal hunger and transitory shocks, as may accompany structural adjustment. This could be achieved through the kinds of projects described in chapter 2, through components of structural or agriculture sectoral adjustment projects, or through what might be called nutrition sectoral adjustment projects, which would have nutrition improvement as their focus.

Projects to improve the availability of food might take the form of targeted subsidy programs in the commercial market, institutional feeding, or efforts to increase the efficiency of the food marketing systems. These projects may in some instances benefit from collaboration with agencies that provide food aid, a substantial but nonfungible foreign assistance resource that has not been adequately integrated into such efforts. (Some countries, particularly in Sub-Saharan Africa, lack transport, storage, and other infrastructural prerequisites to take advantage of available donated food in the amounts they require. Meeting such needs also is an appropriate goal of nutrition projects.)

Third, large-scale delivery of micronutrients—through fortification or supplementation—has opened the possibility of inroads against the diseases and handicaps resulting from vitamin and mineral deficiencies. These approaches are increasingly important as new evidence broadens understanding of the consequences of micronutrient deficiencies.[7] Recent experience in a number of settings has shown that specific nutrient intervention programs, particularly for vitamin A and iodine, can be successful.

Vitamin A deficiency has long been associated with nutritional blindness and the severity of measles. Now recent research suggests that vitamin A control programs can have a demonstrable beneficial effect on morbidity and mortality due to diarrheal and respiratory disease, even in children without clinical signs of the deficiency. Research in Central America has demonstrated that fortified sugar can reduce vitamin A deficiency. Vitamin A has also been given in high-potency periodic doses at reasonable costs (about $0.10 a year per person for capsules). In Bangladesh wide distribution of capsules substantially reduced vitamin A deficiency and prevented an estimated 2,500 cases of blindness each year.

Understanding also has been broadened recently about the subtle effects on mental and behavioral development of even relatively mild iodine deficiencies. For several decades salt fortified with iodine could be used effectively to control endemic goiter and reduce endemic cretinism and deafness. These programs can be highly cost-effective (for example, $0.05 a year per person or $0.20 a year per case of goiter prevented), but are seldom implemented. Many countries that have legislation calling for iodination do not have effective programs. If salt is not centrally processed or deficiencies are severe, an alternative is a mass dose using an intramuscular injection of iodized oil at about five times the annual cost of fortifying salt; protection lasts for three to five years. (Technology for an oral administration of iodine is now available, but at about double the cost and half the years of protection of the injection.)

Evidence has also been accumulating that nutritional anemia, which affects about half of the women and sizable portions of the men and children in developing countries, has consequences beyond the sickness and sluggishness (and the effect on fatigue in physical performance) with which it has been associated. Recent work suggests that nutritional anemia can deleteriously alter brain chemistry and function and thereby influence human behavior itself. Fortunately, a breakthrough in food technology by Indian scientists has made it possible to fortify a nation's salt supply with iron at a cost of $0.05–0.09 a year per person. And older technologies offer opportunities to fortify centrally processed grain products with vitamins and minerals at a cost of about $0.08 a year per person.

Micronutrient supplementation of a more limited scope can often be carried out within health projects. Indeed, pairing delivery of micronutrient supplements with immunization may prove cost-effective, since the target groups of young children overlap; this was done in Brazil in 1986, when vitamin A supplements were distributed as part of a polio campaign. Fortification may be difficult to administer through health projects, however, because the implementing agency is typically outside the health ministry and sometimes even outside the government. This difficulty and the crowded agenda for primary health care may tempt health project designers to bypass fortification programs. Thus, nutrition projects are probably the most appropriate place to bring together the entities and skills required for successful fortification programs. Fortification has such potential for cost-effectiveness that it should not be allowed to slip between organizational cracks.

Future nutrition projects financed by the Bank generally need not include the kinds of food production and food technology components common in early projects. And water supply programs should be undertaken in nutrition projects only if they include the other elements necessary to provide health and nutrition benefits, such as safe water quality and community training on use and maintenance. Most projects should include objectives to change behavior through nutrition communication and education. This is particularly important when people are faced with major changes, such as significant shifts in real income, movement from a subsistence to a cash economy, or migration from rural areas. Social marketing techniques can be used to help define needs and assist communities in designing nutrition messages and setting up education programs. Mass-media concepts can be used in many countries to complement these efforts.[8]

Almost every project should include training, technical assistance, and other actions to help strengthen institutional capacities to analyze, prepare, manage, and evaluate operations. No project should be without an evaluation component.

The main criteria for judging a proposal should be the project's contribution to a sound nutrition plan and its ability to reach—either initially or through later expansion—large numbers of the nutritionally needy. In countries with little nutrition experience emphasis should be on projects that lay the groundwork for more extensive interventions.

Nutrition Content in Other Projects

The malnutrition commonly identified in the Bank's epidemiological analyses as a major cause of mortality and poor health status should be addressed in health and population projects that involve maternal and child health and primary health care. Those projects should normally incorporate growth monitoring and related nutrition education; other actions supportive of breastfeeding, such as training personnel on how to enhance its contraceptive effect; diarrhea control and management; vitamin and mineral supplementation; and selective supplementary feeding for rehabilitating seriously malnourished children. The importance of nutrition among the other objectives must, of course, be assessed for each project. However, in that process—in addition to examining the advantages of including a nutrition component—the main question that must be asked is what the absence of such a component will do to the expected health or fertility outcomes of the project.

Many of the countries in greatest need, particularly those in Sub-Saharan Africa, may not at present be capable of absorbing freestanding nutrition projects, except perhaps projects aimed at increasing their logistical capacity to use food aid. In these countries special efforts should be made to include components in health and population projects and in technical assistance projects for building or strengthening institutions in training, planning, and other areas and for studies leading to the development of nutrition projects.

Preschool programs, such as Brazil's PROAPE, that serve the broad developmental needs of young children are likely to be implemented by the Ministry of Education and its school facilities and staff. As such, they fit logically within education projects. (The PROAPE concept is based in part on the notion that the lack of improvement in the academic performance of children in the past twenty or twenty-five years—in spite of a dramatic growth in investment in primary school education in developing countries—may not be due to the quality of education but to the quality of students.) Food gardens and other agriculturally oriented nutrition interventions such as those in Indonesia, Sergipe, and Colombia would usually best be handled in agricultural and rural development projects.

In rural development, urban development, and education projects, nutrition activities are likely to be successful only where there is a strong political interest in improving nutrition, where the nutrition component would be large enough to merit attention by project officers, and where local managers are capable of implementing multisectoral projects. Experience suggests that nutrition components in these areas should ordinarily be limited to those that either directly relate to basic project objectives or compensate for nutritionally negative changes the project may cause. Exceptions to this general rule would be components that expand programs already under way in the country (and thus would be easier to implement), help develop local capability, or prepare for a future project directed primarily at nutrition.

Analytic Work

Nutrition issues should be given greater emphasis in economic analyses, as well as in agriculture and health sector work. Nutrition sector work should also be intensified, now that more is known about how to do such work. Recent nutrition sector analyses of Bangladesh, China, the Gambia, the Philippines, Rwanda, Zambia, and Zimbabwe, for example, have added to knowledge about the countries and contributed to economic and social policy formulation.

Nutrition-related research is now at the stage where it can focus on specific problems directly linked to operational activities. Initial priority should be given to evaluation of intermediate indicators. These make up a continuum of guideposts—from delivery of services to behavioral change to increases in consumption to improvements in growth. Once managers and evaluators are satisfied that the intended products and services reach the intended beneficiaries, research can proceed more confidently to explore impact on nutrition status.

Research should also study how to reach those in need who are bypassed by current programs, particularly in food-surplus countries with extensive malnutrition, and how agriculture actions that are assumed to be nutritionally beneficial actually affect nutrition.[9] (At a minimum, agriculture projects that contain evaluation components should, when feasible, include changes in food consumption as a measure of performance.)

Special research attention should be given to identifying strategies to combat malnutrition in Sub-Saharan Africa, which presents formidable challenges. Other important research topics, particularly in the context of structural adjustment lending, are the effects on nutrition of current consumer food subsidy programs and the design of programs to increase nutrition effectiveness. Further study should also be made of the longer-range effects of remedial actions (for example, the extent to which an early-age supplementary feeding program, as in Tamil Nadu, affects subsequent educability and productivity) and the priority of nutrition interventions among other interventions intended to improve health status.

Inroads against Malnutrition

An atmosphere of uncertainty has clouded work in nutrition in recent years, in part because economic adjustment issues have crowded nutrition from development agendas and in part because efforts to improve nutrition have not lived up to expectations. But this situation may be changing, sparked by concerns raised by UNICEF and others.[10] Among both donors and countries, awareness is increasing about the importance of recognizing the shock that economic crises and programs to adjust for them can have on nutrition status. Furthermore, recent evaluations of Bank-assisted nutrition projects, particularly in Tamil Nadu, offer encouraging evidence of the benefits of such projects.

The nutrition projects did not do everything they were supposed to do—in the first three projects the objectives were too ambitious—but on balance they clearly have been worth doing. Substantial portions of the projects have been successful, and countries have taken up and enlarged them on their own. More important, these countries are now looking at nutrition in a different way.

In the late 1970s malnutrition was singled out as one of the contributors to the absolute poverty that afflicts hundreds of millions of individuals in developing countries.[11] Economic development is an important part of the effort to offer a way out of poverty. But it is not a sufficient response for alleviating current suffering. The direct efforts by the Bank and other aid agencies to improve nutrition are but small steps toward meeting a vast need. Nonetheless, they show that steps can be taken.

The initial three largely experimental projects, the first fully operational project in Tamil Nadu, which was in a sense the culmination of earlier experience, and the sector and other analytic work concentrated on nutrition have all led to the realization that malnutrition is a problem arising from poverty that need not wait until incomes increase three or four times to be overcome. Making inroads against malnutrition will not be easy, but the Bank's experience in this area shows that measures can be taken that can make a difference.

Bibliographic Notes

Chapter 1

1 Alan Berg, *The Nutrition Factor: Its Role in National Development* (Washington, D.C.: Brookings Institution, 1973).
2 Alan Berg, *Malnourished People: A Policy View* (Washington, D.C.: World Bank, 1981). Also see the writings of Shlomo Reutlinger, many of which are cited in chapter 6.
3 Shlomo Reutlinger and Jack van Holst Pellekaan, *Poverty and Hunger: Issues and Options for Food Security in Developing Countries* (Washington, D.C.: World Bank, 1986).
4 Cecile C. deSweemer, "Growth and Morbidity," Ph.D. dissertation, Johns Hopkins University, 1974. Also see Carl E. Taylor's essay in Alan Berg, Nevin S. Scrimshaw, and David L. Call, eds., *Nutrition, National Development, and Planning* (Cambridge, Mass.: MIT Press, 1973), pp. 92–93.

Chapter 2

1 Miguel Urrutia, *Winners and Losers in Colombia's Economic Growth of the 1970s* (New York: Oxford University Press, 1985).
2 Roberto Moreira Nunes da Silva, "Avaliação Antropométrica do PINS," unpublished report prepared under an agreement between the Brazilian National Food and Nutrition Institute and the World Bank, 1982.
3 From a preliminary evaluation of the Brazil project, undertaken by Peter Knight, in 1982.
4 Mario Ochoa, "The Colombian Food System: Design, Results, National Impact and Political Constraints," draft study prepared for the International Food Policy Research Institute (IFPRI) (Washington, D.C., 1984); and Tomás Uribe-Mosquera, "The Political Economy of PAN," paper prepared for IFPRI (Washington, D.C., 1985).

5 From an evaluation of the PAN program, conducted by Per Pinstrup-Andersen in 1983.

6 Vital Didonet, "Atendimento integrado de educação saúde nutrição, e envolvimento comunitario do pre-escolar, através de metodologia de baixo custo e ampla cobertura: síntese da exposição," paper presented at the World Assembly of Preschool Education, Quebec, August 28–September 2, 1980.

7 From an unpublished paper prepared by Emmerich Schebeck for a 1982 meeting of the United Nations Children's Fund, "Targeted Consumer Food Subsidies versus Targeted Food Marketing Interventions: Myth and Reality"; also discussed in an evaluation of the Rede Somar program, conducted by Pasquale Scandizzo in 1980.

8 Based on interviews conducted during Asok Mitra's site visit to the Tamil Nadu project in 1982.

9 M. K. Bhan, Shanti Ghosh, and others, *Successful Growth Monitoring: Some Lessons from India* (New Delhi: United Nations Children's Fund Regional Office for South Central Asia, 1986).

10 C. Gopalan and Meera Chatterjee, *Use of Growth Charts for Promoting Child Nutrition: A Review of Global Experience,* Special Publication Series 2 (New Delhi: Nutrition Foundation of India, 1985).

11 Bhan, Ghosh, and others, *Successful Growth Monitoring.*

12 Satoto and others, "Nutrition Intervention Pilot Project Evaluation: A Cohort Study of Children in Selected Project and Comparison Villages in Indonesia," Fellowship Paper (Boston: Tufts University, School of Nutrition, 1983).

13 Djumadias Abunain and Abas B. Jahari, "Study on Impact of NIPP in Two Kabupatens" (Bogor, Indonesia: Center for Research and Development in Nutrition, 1984).

14 Peter A. Berman, "Equity and Cost in the Organization of Primary Health Care in Java, Indonesia," Ph.D. dissertation, Cornell University, 1984.

15 World Health Organization, "WHO Inter-Regional Workshop on Breast-feeding and Fertility: Proceedings and Report," report of a workshop held in Singapore in December 1985, Maternal and Child Health Publication 85.14 (Geneva, 1985).

16 World Bank, *World Development Report 1984* (New York: Oxford University Press, 1984).

17 John Bongaarts and Odile Frank, "The Proximate Determinants of Fertility in Sub-Saharan Africa," PHN Technical Note 85-11, World Bank, Population, Health, and Nutrition Department, Washington, D.C., 1985.

18 Dirce Sigulem, "Influences of Feeding Practices on the Nutritional Condition of Nurslings and Preschool Children" (São Paulo, Brazil: Institute of Preventive Medicine, Paulista School of Medicine, 1980).

19 BKKBN (National Family Planning and Coordinating Board); the Universities of Udayana, Brawijaya, and Airlangga; and Community Systems Foundation, KB-Gizi, *An Indonesian Integrated Family Planning, Nutrition and Health Program: The Evaluation of the First Five Years of Program Imple-*

mentation in East Java and Bali (Ann Arbor, Michigan: Community Systems Foundation, 1986).

20 Marcia Griffiths, Richard K. Manoff, Marion Zeitlan, and others, *Nutrition Communication and Behavior Change Component, Indonesia Nutrition Development Program*, 5 vols. (Washington, D.C.: Manoff International, 1980–83). Summaries can be found in Marcia Griffiths, "Nutrition Education's Promise: Can It Be Kept?" in Martin J. Forman, ed., *Nutritional Aspects of Project Food Aid* (Rome: United Nations Administrative Committee on Coordination, Sub-Committee on Nutrition, 1986) and Marcia Griffiths, "Mothers Speak, Nutrition Educators Listen: Formative Evaluation for a Nutrition Communications Project," paper presented at the Twelfth International Congress of Nutrition, San Diego, August 1981.

21 Bhan, Ghosh, and others, *Successful Growth Monitoring*. For the definitive work on the topic, see Marcia Griffiths, *Growth Monitoring of Preschool Children: Practical Considerations for Primary Health Care Projects*, prepared for UNICEF (Washington, D.C.: World Federation of Public Health Associations, 1985).

22 Consuelo Uribe, "Limitations and Constraints of Colombia's Food and Nutrition Plan PAN," *Food Policy*, vol. 2, no. 1 (February 1986), pp. 47–70.

23 From an evaluation of the home and village garden program in NIPP areas, conducted for the Indonesian Ministry of Health by Ika Harimurthi in 1982, also discussed in an unpublished paper prepared by Emmerich Schebeck for a 1982 meeting of the United Nations Children's Fund, "Food Production and Consumption Linkages for the Rural Poor."

24 From an evaluation of the PRAMENSE component in Sergipe, conducted by Judith Tendler in 1979.

25 From an evaluation of the PAN program conducted by Per Pinstrup-Andersen in 1983.

26 Darwin Karyadi and Samir Basta, *Nutrition and Health of Indonesia Construction Workers*, World Bank Staff Working Paper 152 (Washington, D.C., 1973); Samir Basta and Anthony Churchill, *Iron Deficiency and the Productivity of Adult Males in Indonesia*, World Bank Staff Working Paper 175 (Washington, D.C., 1974).

27 Bhan, Ghosh, and others, *Successful Growth Monitoring*.

28 Selo Soemardjan and others, *Evaluation of the Indonesia Nutrition Development Project*, vol. 1: *Report of the Evaluation Team to the Ministry of Health* (Jakarta Ministry of Health, 1982).

29 From the preliminary evaluation of the Brazil project undertaken by Peter Knight in 1982.

Chapter 3

1 George H. Beaton and Hossein Ghassemi, "Supplementary Feeding Programs for Young Children in Developing Countries," report prepared for

UNICEF and the Administrative Committee on Coordination, Sub-Committee on Nutrition (New York: United Nations, 1979), table 12, p. 45. Also published in *American Journal of Clinical Nutrition,* vol. 35 (April 1982), pp. 864-915. Analysis during a nutrition sector mission in 1984 of Bangladesh's institutional feeding program found per child costs there to be $248 a year, most of this however in the form of foreign food donations.

2 From a preliminary cost analysis of the Tamil Nadu project conducted by David Dapice for the World Bank in 1986, based on a preliminary analysis by Reynaldo Martorell of nutrition data from the Tamil Nadu project.

3 Teresa J. Ho, "Economic Issues: Costs, Affordability and Cost-Effectiveness," Technical Note 85-14, World Bank, Population, Health, and Nutrition Department, Washington, D.C., 1983.

4 Ho, "Economic Issues."

5 Beaton and Ghassemi, "Supplementary Feeding Programs."

6 From an unpublished paper prepared by Michael Mills on the cost-effectiveness of food and nutrition intervention programs, prepared as background for the 1984 Bangladesh Food and Nutrition Sector Review conducted by the World Bank.

Chapter 4

1 Consuelo Uribe, "Colombia's Food and Nutrition Plan PAN," *Food Policy,* vol. 12, no. 1 (February 1986), pp. 47-70; and Tomás Uribe-Mosquera, "The Political Economy of PAN," paper prepared for the International Food Policy Research Institute (Washington, D.C., 1985).

2 Uribe, "Colombia's Food and Nutrition Plan"; and Uribe-Mosquera, "Political Economy of PAN."

3 Guido Deboeck and Ronald Ng, *Monitoring Rural Development in East Asia,* World Bank Staff Working Paper 439 (Washington, D.C., 1980).

4 Robert Ayers, *Banking on the Poor: The World Bank and World Poverty* (Cambridge, Mass.: MIT Press, 1983).

Chapter 5

1 Amorn Nondasuta, "We Found a Way to Prevent Serious Malnutrition," *World Health Forum,* vol. 4, no. 1 (1983), pp. 18-20.

2 Sara Millman, "Trends in Breastfeeding in a Dozen Developing Countries," *International Family Planning Perspectives,* vol. 12, no. 3 (September 1986), pp. 91-95.

3 World Bank, *Learning by Doing: World Bank Lending for Urban Development, 1972-82* (Washington, D.C., 1983).

4 Theodore J. Goering, *Agricultural Research: Sector Policy Paper* (Washington, D.C.: World Bank, 1981), p. 41. Also see Per Pinstrup-Andersen, Alan Berg, and Martin Forman, eds., *International Agricultural Research and Human Nutrition* (Washington, D.C.: International Food Policy Research

Institute and United Nations Administrative Committee on Coordination, Sub-Committee on Nutrition, 1984).

5 Nathan Koffsky, "Nutrition in Agriculture Sector Work Guidelines," World Bank, Agriculture and Rural Development and Population, Health, and Nutrition Departments, Washington, D.C., 1982. Also available as part of Technical Note 86-12, cited in footnote 6. Also see Per Pinstrup-Andersen, *Nutritional Consequences of Agricultural Projects: Conceptual Relationships and Assessment Approaches*, World Bank Staff Working Paper 456 (Washington, D.C., 1981) and Shlomo Reutlinger, "Nutritional Impact of Agricultural Projects," World Bank, Agriculture and Rural Development Department Research Unit Discussion Paper 14, Washington, D.C., 1983.

6 Alan Berg and James Austin, "Nutrition Policies and Programmes: A Decade of Redirection," *Food Policy*, vol. 9, no. 4 (November 1984), pp. 304–11. Also see Alan Berg and others, "Guidelines for Work in Nutrition," Technical Note 86-12, World Bank, Population, Health, and Nutrition Department, Washington, D.C., 1986.

7 Anthony Measham, "Review of PHN Sector Work and Lending in Health, 1980–85," World Bank, Population, Health, and Nutrition Department, Washington, D.C., 1986.

Chapter 6

1 From a background paper on nutrition economic and sector work prepared by Robert Muscat for this monograph.

2 From a nutrition sector study on Zimbabwe prepared by World Bank staff in 1982.

3 Shlomo Reutlinger and Marcelo Selowsky, *Malnutrition and Poverty: Magnitude and Policy Options*, World Bank Occasional Paper 23 (Baltimore, Md.: Johns Hopkins University Press, 1976); Shlomo Reutlinger and Harold Alderman, "The Prevalence of Calorie-Deficient Diets in Developing Countries," *World Development*, vol. 8 (1980), pp. 399–411, also reprinted as World Bank Reprint 158.

4 Marcelo Selowsky, *Balancing Trickle Down and Basic Needs Strategies: Income Distribution Issues in Large Middle-Income Countries, with Special Reference to Latin America*, World Bank Staff Working Paper 335 (Washington, D.C., 1979).

5 Michael Lipton, *Poverty, Undernutrition, and Hunger*, World Bank Staff Working Paper 597 (Washington, D.C., 1983); T. N. Srinivasan, "Malnutrition: Some Measurement and Policy Issues," *Journal of Development Economics*, vol. 8 (1981), pp. 3–19, also reprinted as World Bank Reprint 178. Their work is based on ideas developed in P. V. Sukhatme, "Malnutrition and Poverty," Ninth Lal Bahadur Shastri Memorial Lecture, Indian Agricultural Research Institute, New Delhi, January 27, 1977; Food and Agriculture Organization, *Fourth World Food Survey*, FAO Nutrition Report Series 10 (Rome, 1977); and Food and Agriculture Organization, *Agriculture: Toward 2000*, FAO Conference Report 79/24 (Rome, 1979).

6 Odin Knudsen and Pasquale Scandizzo, *Nutrition and Food Needs in Developing Countries,* World Bank Staff Working Paper 328 (Washington, D.C., 1979).
7 Alan Berg, *Malnourished People: A Policy View* (Washington, D.C.: World Bank, 1981); Shlomo Reutlinger, "Malnutrition: A Poverty or a Food Problem?" *World Development,* vol. 5, no. 8 (August 1977), pp. 715–24, also reprinted as World Bank Reprint 47.
8 Lani S. Stephenson, Michael C. Latham, and S. S. Basta, *The Nutritional and Economic Implications of Ascaris Infection in Kenya,* World Bank Staff Working Paper 271 (Washington, D.C., 1977).
9 Arnfried Keilman and others, *Child and Maternal Health Services in Rural India: The Narangwal Experiment,* vol. 1: *Integrated Nutrition and Health Care* (Baltimore, Md.: Johns Hopkins University Press, 1983).
10 Davidson R. Gwatkin, Janet R. Wilcox, and Joe D. Wray, "Can Nutrition Efforts Make a Difference?" in Berg, *Malnourished People,* app. C, a summary of a report to the World Bank, which was also published in revised form as *Can Health and Nutrition Interventions Make a Difference?,* by the Overseas Development Council, Washington, D.C.
11 Samir S. Basta and Anthony Churchill, *Iron Deficiency Anemia and the Productivity of Adult Males in Indonesia,* World Bank Staff Working Paper 175 (Washington, D.C., 1974). Also see Samir S. Basta, Darwin Karyadi, Soekirman, and Nevin S. Scrimshaw, "Iron Deficiency Anemia and the Productivity of Adult Males in Indonesia," *American Journal of Clinical Nutrition,* vol. 32, no. 4 (April 1979), pp. 916–25.
12 Michael C. Latham and Lani S. Stephenson, "Kenya: Health, Nutrition, and Worker Productivity Studies," World Bank, Population, Health, and Nutrition Department, Washington, D.C., 1981; a portion of this work appears in a separate article, "Costs, Prevalence and Approaches for Control of Ascaris Infection in Kenya," *Journal of Tropical Pediatrics,* no. 26 (December 1980), pp. 246–64.
13 "Effect of Health and Nutrition Status of Road Construction Workers in Northern India on Productivity," Technical Memorandum 4, World Bank Urban Projects Department, Washington, D.C., 1975.
14 Henry M. Levin, "A Benefit-Cost Analysis of Anemia Reduction," Technical Note 85-12, World Bank, Population, Health, and Nutrition Department, Washington, D.C., 1985. Also see Susan Horton and Timothy King, *Labor Productivity: Un Tour d'Horizon,* World Bank Staff Working Paper 497 (Washington, D.C., 1981).
15 Joanne Leslie and Peter R. Moock, "Childhood Malnutrition and Schooling in the Terai Region of Nepal," Discussion Paper 17, World Bank, Education and Training Department, Washington, D.C., 1985.
16 Dean T. Jamison, "Child Malnutrition and School Performance in China," Discussion Paper 17, World Bank, Education and Training Department, Washington, D.C., 1985.
17 Marie Helene Benecio D'Aquino and others, "Avaliação Antropométrica de Eficácia da Suplementação do Pre-Escolar," *Revista de Saúde Publica,* vol. 15, supp. (December 1981), pp. 40–47.
18 From a consultancy report by M. G. Herrera and C. M. Super on school

performance and physical growth of underprivileged children in the Bogotá Project, 1983.

19 Odin K. Knudsen, *Economics of Supplemental Feeding of Malnourished Children: Leakages, Costs, and Benefits,* World Bank Staff Working Paper 451 (Washington, D.C., 1981).

20 Pasquale L. Scandizzo and Judith Graves, "The Alleviation of Malnutrition: Impact and Cost-Effectiveness of Official Programs," AGREP Division Working Paper 19, World Bank, Agriculture and Rural Development Department, Washington, D.C., 1981.

21 Pasquale L. Scandizzo and Gurushri Swamy, *Benefits and Costs of Food Distribution Policies: The India Case,* World Bank Staff Working Paper 509 (Washington, D.C., 1982).

22 Paul Isenman, "Basic Needs: The Case of Sri Lanka," *World Development,* vol. 8 (March 1980), pp. 237–58.

23 Marcelo Selowsky, "Food Prices and the Indexing of the Food Stamp Program in Sri Lanka: An Evaluation of the Trade-offs," World Bank, Washington, D.C., 1980.

24 Edward Clay and others, *Food Policy Issues in Low-Income Countries,* World Bank Staff Working Paper 473 (Washington, D.C., 1980).

25 From a report on the nutritional consequences of agricultural development projects, prepared by Terence II. Martin for the World Bank in 1983.

26 Harold Alderman, Roger Slade, and Per Pinstrup-Andersen are presently preparing a publication on this issue based on collaborative research by the World Bank and the International Food Policy Research Institute, Washington, D.C.

27 Per Pinstrup-Andersen, *Nutritional Consequences of Agricultural Projects: Conceptual Relationships and Assessment Approaches,* World Bank Staff Working Paper 456 (Washington, D.C., 1981). Also see Pasquale Scandizzo, "Analyzing Nutrition Effects of Agricultural Projects," Interim Guidance Note 7, World Bank, Agriculture and Rural Development Department, Washington, D.C., 1981.

28 Reutlinger and Selowsky, *Malnutrition and Poverty.*

29 Lloyd Harbert and Pasquale L. Scandizzo, *Food Distribution and Nutrition Intervention: The Case of Chile,* World Bank Staff Working Paper 512 (Washington, D.C., 1982).

30 Marcelo Selowsky, *Economic Dimensions of Malnutrition in Young Children: A Survey of the Issues,* World Bank Staff Working Paper 294 (Washington, D.C., 1978).

31 Dennis H. Wood and Christopher J. Roesel, "Analysis of Government Costs of Selected Strategies to Achieve Minimum Calorie Standards for a Defined Target Group in Three Developing Countries," background paper for World Bank, *World Development Report 1982* (New York: Oxford University Press, 1982).

32 Selowsky, *Balancing Trickle Down and Basic Needs Strategies.*

33 Lyn Squire and Herman G. van der Tak, *Economic Analysis of Projects* (Baltimore, Md.: Johns Hopkins University Press, 1975).

34 Pasquale L. Scandizzo and Odin K. Knudsen, "The Evaluation of the Benefits of Basic Needs Policies," *American Journal of Agricultural Econom-*

ics, vol. 62 (February 1980), pp. 46–57; Knudsen, *Economics of Supplemental Feeding of Malnourished Children*.

35 Pinstrup-Andersen, *Nutritional Consequences of Agricultural Projects*.

36 Shlomo Reutlinger, "Nutritional Impact of Agricultural Projects," paper prepared for the United Nations Administrative Committee on Coordination, Sub-Committee on Nutrition, Workshop on Nutrition in Agriculture and Rural Development Projects, Castelgandolfo, Italy, February 1983.

37 Odin K. Knudsen and Pasquale L. Scandizzo, "The Demand for Calories in Developing Countries," *American Journal of Agricultural Economics*, vol. 64 (February 1982), pp. 80–86.

38 Dov Chernichovsky and Oey Astra Meesook, *Patterns of Food Consumption and Nutrition in Indonesia: An Analysis of the National Socioeconomic Survey, 1978*, World Bank Staff Working Paper 670 (Washington, D.C., 1985).

39 Peter T. Knight, Dennis Mahar, and Ricardo Moran, "Health, Nutrition and Education," in *Brazil: Human Resources Special Report* (Washington, D.C.: World Bank, 1979), annex 3; Rakesh Mohan, M. Wilhelm Wagner, and Jorge García, *Measuring Urban Malnutrition and Poverty: A Case Study of Bogotá and Cali, Colombia*, World Bank Staff Working Paper 447 (Washington, D.C., 1981); Joanne Leslie, Reynaldo Martorell, and Peter R. Moock, "Characteristics and Determinants of Child Nutritional Status in Nepal," Discussion Paper 82-15, World Bank, Population, Health, and Nutrition Department, Population and Human Resources Division, Washington, D.C., 1982; Dean T. Jamison, Teresa J. Ho, and F. L. Trowbridge, "Food Availability and the Nutritional Status of Children in China," Discussion Paper 81-26, World Bank, Population, Health, and Nutrition Department, Washington, D.C., 1981; Alan L. Piazza, *Trends in Food and Nutrient Availability in China, 1950–81*, World Bank Staff Working Paper 607 (Washington, D.C., 1983); Ramesh Chander, Christiaan Grootaert, and Graham Pyatt, *Living Standards Surveys in Developing Countries*, World Bank Living Standards Measurement Study Working Paper 1 (Washington, D.C., 1980); Reynaldo Martorell, *Nutrition and Health Status Indicators: Suggestions for Surveys of the Standard of Living in Developing Countries*, World Bank Living Standards Measurement Study Working Paper 13 (Washington, D.C., 1982).

40 Martorell, *Nutrition and Health Status Indicators*.

41 Growth chart developed by Marcia Griffiths and Alan Berg. See *Mothers and Children*, vol. 6, no. 1 (Washington, D.C.: American Public Health Association, 1987), p. 7.

42 Oscar Echeverri, Population, Health and Nutrition Department, forthcoming.

43 Howard N. Barnum and Lyn Squire, *A Model of an Agricultural Household: Theory and Evidence*, World Bank Staff Occasional Paper 27 (Baltimore, Md.: Johns Hopkins University Press, 1979); Dov Chernichovsky, "An Economic Theory of the Household and Impact Measurement of Nutrition and Related Health Programs," in Robert E. Klein, ed., *Evaluating the Impact of Nutrition and Health Programs* (New York: Plenum, 1979); Inderjit Singh and Lyn Squire, "A Model of the Agricultural Household: Some Implications for Nutrition Policies in Rural Areas," paper presented at the

Conference on the Economics of Nutrition-Oriented Food Policies and Programs, Bellagio, Italy, September 1978.

44 Eileen T. Kennedy and Bruce Cogill, "Income and Nutritional Effects of the Commercialization of Agriculture: The Case of Kenya," IFPRI Research Report (Washington, D.C.: International Food Policy Research Institute, forthcoming).

45 Alan Berg and others, "Nutrition," in National Research Council, Commission on International Relations, *World Food and Nutrition Study: Supporting Papers*, vol. 4 (Washington, D.C.: National Academy of Sciences, 1977), also published by the U.S. Senate Committee on Nutrition, 95th Cong., 2 Sess., U.S. Government Printing Office, Washington, D.C., 1977); Shlomo Reutlinger, "Nutritional Cost-Effectiveness Considerations," in National Research Council, Committee on International Nutrition Programs, *Nutritional Analysis of Public Law 480 Title II Commodities* (Washington, D.C.: National Academy of Sciences, 1982), pp. 54–107. Also see Shlomo Reutlinger, "Project Food Aid and Equitable Growth: Income Transfer Efficiency First!" Discussion Paper ARU-13, World Bank, Agriculture and Rural Development Department, Washington, D.C., 1983.

46 The first to be published is Robert C. Hornik, *Nutrition Education: A State-of-the-Art Review*, Nutrition Policy Discussion Paper 9 (Rome: United Nations Administrative Committee on Coordination, Sub-Committee on Nutrition, 1985); others by Teresa J. Ho and Terence H. Martin, forthcoming.

Chapter 7

1 Marcia Griffiths, "Nutrition Education's Promise: Can It Be Kept?" in Martin J. Forman, ed., *Nutritional Aspects of Project Food Aid* (Rome: United Nations Administrative Committee on Coordination, Sub-Committee on Nutrition, 1986); also see her "Growth Monitoring and Nutrition Education," in Christine Hollis, ed., *Using Communications to Solve Nutrition Problems, A Compendium* (Newton, Mass.: International Nutrition Communication Service, Education Development Center, 1986).

2 John P. Kevany, "The Tamil Nadu Integrated Nutrition Project: Training and Education," *NFI Bulletin*, Nutrition Foundation of India, vol. 7, no. 4 (October 1986).

3 Vital Didonet, "Atendimento integrado de educação saúde nutrição, e envolvimento comunitario do pre-escolar, através de metodologia de baixo custo e ampla cobertura: síntese da exposição," paper presented at the World Assembly of Preschool Education, Quebec, August 28–September 2, 1980.

Chapter 8

1 Shlomo Reutlinger and Jack van Holst Pellekaan, *Poverty and Hunger: Issues and Options for Food Security in Developing Countries* (Washington, D.C.: World Bank, 1986).

2 Yukon Huang and Peter Nicholas, "The Social Cost of Adjustment," *Finance and Development*, vol. 24, no. 2 (June 1987), pp. 22–25, and Roberto Becker and Aaron Lechtig, "Increasing Poverty and Infant Mortality in the Northeast of Brazil," *Journal of Tropical Pediatrics*, forthcoming.

3 Per Pinstrup-Andersen, "Macroeconomic Adjustment Policies and Human Nutrition: Available Evidence and Research Needs," paper prepared for the Administrative Committee on Coordination, Sub-Committee on Nutrition, Twelfth Session, Tokyo, April 1986. See also Pinstrup-Andersen, "Assuring Food Security and Adequate Nutrition for the Poor during Periods of Economic Crisis and Macroeconomic Adjustments: Policy Options and Experience with Food Subsidies and Transfer Programs," paper prepared for the Second Takemi Symposium on International Health, Harvard University, Cambridge, Mass., May 1986. For a discussion of options and experience in targeting, see Alan Berg, *Malnourished People: A Policy View* (Washington, D.C.: World Bank, 1981).

4 Pinstrup-Andersen, "Macroeconomic Adjustment Policies and Human Nutrition" and "Assuring Food Security and Adequate Nutrition."

5 Anthony Measham, "Review of PHN Sector Work and Lending in Health, 1980–85," Technical Note 86-14, World Bank, Population, Health, and Nutrition Department, Washington, D.C., 1986.

6 Fred Sai, "Keynote Address to the All-Africa Parliamentary Conference on Population and Development," Harare, Zimbabwe, May 1986.

7 Alan Berg and Susan Brems, "Micronutrient Deficiencies: Present Knowledge on Effects and Control," Technical Note 86-32, World Bank, Population, Health, and Nutrition Department, Washington, D.C., 1986.

8 Richard K. Manoff, *Social Marketing: New Imperative for Public Health* (New York: Praeger, 1985), and Marcia Griffiths, "A Case for an Anthropological Perspective in Nutrition Education Materials Design," paper presented at the American Anthropological Association annual conference, Washington, D.C., December 1982.

9 From a report on the nutritional consequences of agricultural development projects, prepared by Terence H. Martin for the World Bank in 1983.

10 Giovanni Andrea Cornia, Richard Jolly, and Frances Stewart, *Adjustment with a Human Face: Protecting the Vulnerable and Promoting Growth* (New York: Oxford University Press, 1987).

11 Robert S. McNamara, preface to Berg, *Malnourished People.*

Index

World Health Organization (WHO), 28, 85, 122 n15

Wray, Joe D., 126 n10

Yemen, People's Democratic Republic of, 73

Yemen Arab Republic, 72, 73, 80, 82

Zambia, 6, 80, 81, 82, 88, 119
Zeitlan, Marion, 123 n20
Zimbabwe, 6, 80, 82, 85, 119